Hospitality &
Human Services

Daniel Lewis

MASON CREST

Mason Crest
450 Parkway Drive, Suite D
Broomall, PA 19008
www.masoncrest.com

Printed in the United States of America
First printing
9 8 7 6 5 4 3 2 1

Series ISBN: 978-1-4222-4132-5
Hardcover ISBN: 978-1-4222-4138-7

Library of Congress Cataloging-in-Publication Data is available on file.

Developed and Produced by Print Matters Productions, Inc.
(www.printmattersinc.com)
Cover and Interior Design by Lori S Malkin Design, LLC

CAREERS IN DEMAND FOR HIGH SCHOOL GRADUATES

Agriculture, Food & Natural Resources

Armed Forces

Computers, Communications & the Arts

Construction & Trades

Fitness, Personal Care Services & Education

Health Care & Science

Hospitality & Human Services

Public Safety & Law

Sales, Marketing & Finance

Transportation & Manufacturing

KEY ICONS TO LOOK FOR:

 Words to understand: These words with their easy-to-understand definitions will increase the reader's understanding of the text while building vocabulary skills.

 Sidebars: This boxed material within the main text allows readers to build knowledge, gain insights, explore possibilities, and broaden their perspectives by weaving together additional information to provide realistic and holistic perspectives.

 Educational Videos: Readers can view videos by scanning our QR codes, providing them with additional educational content to supplement the text. Examples include news coverage, moments in history, speeches, iconic sports moments and much more!

 Text-dependent Questions: These questions send the reader back to the text for more careful attention to the evidence presented there.

 Research projects: Readers are pointed toward areas of further inquiry connected to each chapter. Suggestions are provided for projects that encourage deeper research and analysis.

CONTENTS

For millions of Americans, life after high school means stepping into the real world. Each year more than 1 million of the nation's 3.1 million high school graduates go directly into the workforce. Clearly, college isn't for everyone. Many people learn best by using their hands rather than by sitting in a classroom. Others find that the escalating cost of college puts it beyond reach, at least for the time being. During the 2016–2017 school year, for instance, tuition and fees at a "moderate" four-year, in-state public college averaged $24,610, not including housing costs, according to The College Board.

The good news is that there's a wide range of exciting, satisfying careers available without a four-year bachelor's degree or even a two-year associate's degree. Careers in Demand for High School Graduates highlights specific, in-demand careers in which individuals who have only a high school diploma or the general educational development (GED) credential can find work, with or without further training (outside of college).

These jobs span the range from apprentice electronics technician to chef, teacher's assistant, Web page designer, sales associate, and lab technician. The additional training that some of these positions require may be completed either on the job, through a certificate program, or during an apprenticeship that combines entry-level work and class time. Happily, there's plenty of growth in the number of jobs that don't require a college diploma, though that growth is fastest for positions that call for additional technical training or a certificate of proficiency.

So, what career should a high school graduate consider? The range is so broad that Careers in Demand for High School Graduates includes 10 volumes, each based on related career fields from the Department of Labor's career clusters. Within each volume approximately 10 careers are profiled, encouraging readers to focus on a wide selection of job possibilities, some of which readers may not even know exist. To enable readers to narrow their choices, each chapter offers a self-assessment quiz that helps answer the question, "Is this career for me?" What's more, each job profile includes an insightful look at what the position involves, highlights of a typical day, insight into the work environment, and an interview with someone on the job.

An essential part of the decision to enter a particular field includes how much additional training is needed. Careers in Demand features opportunities that require no further academic study or training beyond high school as well as those that do. Readers in high school can start prepping for careers immediately through volunteer work, internships, academic classes, technical programs, or career academies. (Currently, for instance, one in four students concentrates on a vocational or technical program.) For each profile, the best ways for high school students to prepare are featured in a "Start Preparing Now" section.

For readers who are called to serve in the armed forces, this decision also provides an opportunity to step into a range of careers. Every branch of the armed forces, from the army to the coast guard, offers training in areas including administrative, construction, electronics, health care, and protective services. One volume of Careers in Demand for High School Graduates is devoted to careers that can be reached with military training. These range from personnel specialist to aircraft mechanic.

Beyond military options, other entry-level careers provide job seekers with an opportunity to test-drive a career without a huge commitment. Compare the ease of switching from being a bank teller to a sales representative, for instance, with that of investing three years and tens of thousands of dollars into a law school education, only to discover a dislike for the profession. This series offers not only a look at related careers but also ways to advance in the field. Another section, "Finding a Job," provides job-hunting tips specific to each career. This includes, for instance, advice for teacher assistants to develop a portfolio of their work. As it turns out, employers of entry-level workers aren't looking for degrees and academic achievements. They want employability skills: a sense of responsibility, a willingness to learn, discipline, flexibility, and above all, enthusiasm. Luckily, with 100 jobs profiled in Careers in Demand for High School Graduates, finding the perfect one to get enthusiastic about is easier than ever.

In this volume, you will be introduced to an exciting array of careers in the hospitality industry. Many of the jobs featured in this volume offer flexible hours and part-time work, but what really sets this volume—and indeed this industry—apart from the rest are the unique and diverse places where you can find work. Anywhere people go for leisure, there are jobs to be had at hotels, restaurants, and bars—not to mention at baseball stadiums.

There's Room for You in Hospitality

All hospitality jobs share a common purpose: to service people in the best way. Every job is designed to make people's lives a bit brighter, whether it's by preparing an exquisite meal, making sure someone's flight is enjoyable, or putting together a beautiful bouquet of flowers.

It's a fun and fast-paced industry filled with jobs that affect people's lives in a positive way, so if you enjoy working in crowded environments, and have a friendly or outgoing disposition, this may be the field for you.

If you are new to the hospitality industry or you've never worked before, one of the easiest places to land a job is the food and beverage industry. Not only is it the nation's largest employer outside of the government, but it's also known for hiring young and inexperienced workers. According to the National Restaurant Association, about one in three adults got their first job experience in a restaurant. So if you enjoy cooking and can handle fast-paced environments, the first job profiled in this volume may pique your interest.

Cooks and food-prep workers spend a lot of time on their feet and often have to cook or prepare more than a hundred meals per day. The work can be stressful and demanding, but if you can handle the pressure of sautéing onions, chopping vegetables, and cooking salmon all at the same time, then you might really enjoy working in a kitchen for a living. Check out chapter 3 for more information.

On the other hand, if you love the atmosphere of restaurants, but your idea of cooking is popping a frozen entrée into the microwave, then you should consider working in what is called the front end of the restaurant. Chapter 4 profiles the responsibilities of waiters, waitresses, hosts, and hostesses. The work can be just as stressful, but instead of searing scallops and lifting large pots of boiling water, waiters and hosts make sure that the customers are satisfied and everything is running smoothly.

In order to work in the front end, you must be fast on your feet and friendly. If this sounds interesting, you should also check out Chapter 5, which profiles bartenders. Although some bartenders work in the front end of restaurants, they're more frequently found in late-night establishments, such as bars, clubs, and lounges. This job requires more training than that of a waiter or even a food-prep worker because not only do you need to know how to mix hundreds of drinks, but you also have to be skilled at dealing with disturbances caused by drunken patrons.

If the food service industry sounds too fast-paced for your liking, then the hospitality jobs featured in Chapters 6 and 7 might be more your speed. Floral arrangers and dry cleaning workers typically work in small, quiet environments. Though their clientele can be just as demanding, both floral arrangers and dry cleaners create their own deadlines and work at a pace that is comfortable for them. If you're at all artistically inclined, you might really enjoy the art of picking flowers and arranging bouquets and displays. With customers who may return every week, successful dry cleaners are organized and personable.

One of the greatest aspects of the hospitality industry is that there are plenty of opportunities to run your own business. Many careers profiled in the chapters of this book can lead to management or ownership positions if you stick it out and work hard. At many hospitality jobs, the managers value experience as much as—if not more than—a college education. The industry is built on ambition and hard work, which is part of the reason why it attracts so many entrepreneurs and go-getters. It is not uncommon to hear of young people taking the money that they would have spent on college and investing it in their own restaurant, bar, bed-and-breakfast, or florist shop.

If you're interested in opening your own business, keep in mind that it requires more than just "people skills." You must be sharp, good with numbers, and have excellent leadership and management skills. These skills can be hard to develop without any guidance, which is why this book gives you advice on how to sharpen your business acumen through classes, seminars, internships, certifications, and part-time work. Although some of the jobs call for more formal training, every job in this volume essentially requires the same thing: hard work and gumption.

If travel interests you, then you should definitely read the profile on flight attendants in Chapter 1. This is one of the more exciting and cosmopolitan jobs featured in this volume. You get to travel and meet new people, and it's hard to beat the benefits—free flights to wherever you want and an excellent health and retirement program. That said, the actual job is not as easy as most smiling flight attendants make it look. The hours are long, you're away from home a lot, and the safety of every passenger is in your hands. In addition, the application and training process is intense, so if you're really considering the job, be sure to carefully read the section "Training and How to Get It."

If you would prefer a job that's closer to home and doesn't require as much training, you might want to read Chapter 2, which profiles desk clerks, concierges, and reservation agents. Like flight attendants, these three jobs require you to deal with a revolving door of international customers, many of whom have been traveling all day and are tired or irritable. Their satisfaction and safety is one of your primary responsibilities.

However, unlike flight attendants, these three positions require little or no experience and training. More important, employers in these fields often hire high school students on a part-time basis. So even if these jobs are not the perfect fit for you, working as a desk clerk, concierge, or reservation agent is a great stepping-stone to other jobs in and outside of the hospitality industry. If it's high stakes, suspense, and spontaneity that you're after, then take a look at Chapter 8, which presents the work of professional umpires. More so than the other jobs in this volume, this profession carries a tremendous amount of on-the-spot

▲ Among the duties of a flight attendant is ensuring the safety of all passengers.

pressure. The integrity of every baseball game rests on the umpire's shoulders. The job is so critical to the sport that several umpires have even been admitted into the Baseball Hall of Fame. But before you start dreaming of your own baseball card, the road to the major leagues is long, and only a select few make it. If you're not deterred by the extensive training requirements after reading Chapter 8, pick up a Major League Baseball rule book and start studying.

Unlike other industries, hospitality employers aren't necessarily looking for good grades or fancy degrees. What they value most is employability skills: commitment, responsibility, a willingness to learn, flexibility, and above all, enthusiasm. Some careers require more initial training than others, but with hard work, every job in this volume—and others in the rich universe of hospitality, human services, and tourism that we have not sampled here—is obtainable. And if you stick with it, they can lead you to a satisfying and lucrative career.

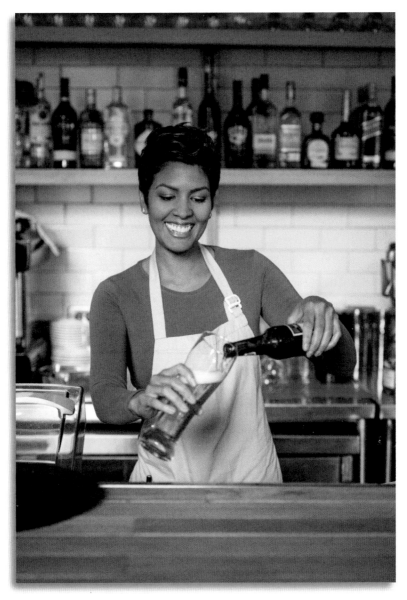

▲ Most bartenders work behind a bar where they serve and interact with patrons. You should be friendly and outgoing, particularly if you want good tips.

Flight Attendant

Travel the world. Meet interesting and diverse people.
Shape passengers' flying experiences.

1

WORDS TO UNDERSTAND

circadian rhythm: the cycle that tells the human body when it's time to sleep.

fractional aircraft: a situation in which multiple parties share ownership of an airplane.

regulations: rules made by a particular authority, such as the Federal Aviation Administration (FAA).

Imagine traveling all across the continent or throughout the world. Flight attendants get these exciting opportunities. What's more, they also meet a huge range of passengers, from parents flying internationally to meet a soon-to-be adopted infant to a chief executive on his or her way to a multimillion-dollar deal. A flight attendant's job is to keep everyone on board safe and comfortable. Though passengers may be mainly aware of their flight attendants' duties pointing out emergency exits and making sure that carry-on items are properly stowed, in fact that's just a small part of what they do. They are an important part of air security and have a serious job that requires patience, endurance, and energy. As it happens, the benefits are enticing. Flight attendants receive plenty of time off, and they and their family members often enjoy no-cost or discounted airfare, allowing attendants to travel widely in their free time.

◀ Flight attendants have a serious job that requires patience, endurance, and energy, but if you love to travel, the benefits are great.

Is This Job Right for You?

To find out if being a flight attendant is a good fit for you, read each of the following questions and answer "Yes" or "No."

Yes	*No*	**1.**	*Do you like to travel, and are you comfortable with flying?*
Yes	*No*	**2.**	*Do you remain calm under duress?*
Yes	*No*	**3.**	*Are you poised, patient, and presentable?*
Yes	*No*	**4.**	*Can you assert yourself and take charge when necessary?*
Yes	*No*	**5.**	*Do you enjoy talking to strangers?*
Yes	*No*	**6.**	*Do you prefer a varied work schedule?*
Yes	*No*	**7.**	*Are you a good listener?*
Yes	*No*	**8.**	*Do you enjoy working on your feet, and are you physically fit?*
Yes	*No*	**9.**	*Could you work in a confined space for long stretches of time?*
Yes	*No*	**10.**	*Are you interested in the well-being and comfort of others?*

If you answered "Yes" to most of the questions, you may have what it takes to be a flight attendant. To find out more about this profession, read on.

What's the Work Like?

Regardless of what airline you work for, a flight attendant's primary responsibility is to ensure the safety of his or her passengers. Airlines are required by law to enforce certain safety **regulations**, such as fastening seat belts and making sure that there is no smoking on board. It is the flight attendant's job to ensure that all in-flight rules and regulations are followed.

Flight attendants spend a considerable amount of time providing customers with drinks and duty-free items, so passengers tend to forget the importance of a flight attendant's job. In many ways, flight attendants are the unsung heroes of the air. During rough weather conditions, they care for sick or anxious passengers. They also administer

TALKING MONEY

Flight attendants earn a median salary of $48,500, according to 2016 data from the U.S. Bureau of Labor Statistics. However, the pay scale for flight attendants varies greatly by carrier and a flight attendant's level of experience. The lowest-paid attendants earned less than of $26,570, while the highest-paid 10 percent of flight attendants made more than $78,650.

▲ Although safety videos are common on large planes, flight attendants on smaller planes will still need to demonstrate safety procedures.

first aid to passengers who become ill onboard, and if the pilots need to make an emergency landing, it is the attendants who direct the evacuation.

In addition to serving the passengers and making sure that safety procedures are being followed, flight attendants have paperwork and administrative tasks to fulfill. Prior to landing, attendants must take inventory of headsets, alcoholic beverages, and moneys collected. They must also write a quick report detailing the condition of the cabin, any items left behind, and if there were any incidents or medical problems onboard. If you thought that a flight attendant's job was just to look good and pour coffee, you might want to think again.

Who's Hiring?

- Commercial airline companies, such as Delta, American Airlines, or Virgin Air.

- **Fractional aircraft** companies, such as NetJets, which specialize in timeshare planes.

- Major corporations and companies, which operate aircraft for business purposes.

▲ Flight attendants spend a considerable amount of time providing customers with food and drinks.

Where Are the Jobs?

It goes without saying that flight attendants spend a significant portion of their workday confined in an aircraft. Because airlines fly 24/7, flight attendants may work nights, holidays, and weekends. Scheduled on-duty time is usually limited to 12 hours per day, but it can be longer if you work for an international carrier.

In addition to the time spent in flight, attendants generally spend about 50 hours a month on the ground preparing planes for flights, writing reports, and waiting for planes to arrive. Generally speaking, flight attendants will work three-day sequences and then receive three or four days off. You can use this time to start a second business or take advantage of the incredible travel benefits that airlines offer flight attendants.

As far as housing is concerned, airlines will assign you to one of their home bases, so most flight attendants choose to live in a town or city that's near to their assigned base. Since home bases and routes are chosen on a seniority basis, the longer you've been employed, the more likely you are to receive your desired route. Most beginning flight attendants work on call, which means that they must be willing to relocate in a relatively short period of time.

This job requires you to be flexible with your hours and to be willing to relocate. It can also be exhausting, but most attendants feel that the job is worth it. Not only does the job offer you great traveling opportunities, but as a flight attendant you are the most visible representative of airline companies. Airlines count on you to build customer relations and maintain their image.

A Typical Day

Here are the highlights of a typical flight attendant's day.

Meet with other crew members. The captain will gather you and your fellow flight attendants to go over such details as the approximate length of the flight, expected weather conditions, and special issues having to do with passengers.

▲ A flight attendant walks down the aisle, checking all overhead bins, ensuring that they are not overstuffed and are securely latched.

Direct the boarding of the craft. You'll greet passengers, check their tickets, and tell them where to store carry-on items. You'll also give the emergency equipment demonstration, and check to see that seatbelts are fastened, seat backs are in upright positions, and all carry-on items are properly stowed.

Serve simple needs and be ready for more. You'll provide passengers with in-flight meals, drinks, duty-free items, and headsets for in-flight entertainment. If there is an injury on board or someone falls ill, the passengers are your responsibility.

Start Preparing Now

- Learn as much as you can about in-flight safety.

- Pay attention in language class! Flight attendants interested in working for international airlines must speak at least one foreign language.

- Hiring policies differ from airline to airline, so it's a good idea to search the Web sites of individual airlines to check out their job opportunities and application requirements.

Training and How to Get It

Although a high school diploma or its equivalent is technically all that's required to enter a flight attendant training program, airlines increasingly prefer applicants with customer service experience or some degree of postsecondary education.

If you're planning to take classes toward an associate's or bachelor's degree before becoming a flight attendant, airlines look for applicants who have studied public service disciplines such as psychology, communications, social studies, or education. Studying a foreign language will also set you apart from the competition. Airlines actively recruit bilingual applicants.

For those who do not wish to start an associate's or bachelor's degree, there are training schools and online programs that offer courses on becoming a flight attendant. The objective of these courses is to go over basic in-flight safety procedures and prepare students for the rigorous application process that airlines impose on flight attendant applicants.

One of the most rigorous parts of the application process is the background check, which the FAA (Federal Aviation Administration) now requires of all applicants. Everything about an applicant is investigated, including date of birth, employment history, criminal record, school records, and gaps in employment. If an applicant's background check reveals any major inconsistencies, an applicant will not be offered a job or will be immediately dismissed from the training program.

NOTES FROM THE FIELD

Flight attendant, New York, New York

Q: *How did you get your job?*

A: I walked into a Delta ticket office in New York City. At the office, they had me fill out an application, and then I flew to Atlanta for an interview with both Delta's people and a psychiatrist (they like to make sure that you aren't unstable). The rest is history.

Q: *What do you like best about your job?*

A: The best part is the people and the amazing travel opportunities. Being involved with the airline industry is not just a job, it's a lifestyle. I'm gone from home quite a bit, but the people I work with have a wonderful sense of adventure. I feel very fortunate to be able to visit places like Paris, Rome, and Mumbai. I also really enjoy the fact that we work in an environment where no one is looking over your shoulder.

Q: *What's the most challenging part of your job?*

A: Onboard, long flights can be stressful, especially when you're in tight quarters or a passenger has had too much to drink. Alcohol has a much stronger effect on people at higher altitudes, and once in a while people get out of control. After September 11, 2001, traveling has become more difficult for everyone, and the airport scene can be particularly stressful. Another challenge is dealing with jetlag. When you disrupt your circadian rhythm on a regular basis, it can wreak havoc on your sleep cycle. I have become an expert at taking power naps. Exercise also helps.

Q: *What are the keys to success to being a flight attendant?*

A: Success in this field involves a sense of humor and flexibility. At 35,000 feet, you have to be creative and quick to solve problems as they arise. People will present you with all kinds of situations, and, while it's important to take their needs seriously, you also need to find humor in some of the more difficult demands.

After passing the interview and background checks, applicants are entered into the airline's flight attendant training program, which can take three to eight weeks. Training programs differ from airline to airline, but every program covers fundamental emergency procedures, such as how to evacuate an airplane, administer first aid, survive in the water, and handle a terrorist situation. Before graduating from the program, you must successfully complete emergency and nonemergency drills. Once you accomplish all this, you will officially receive a certificate of demonstrated proficiency from the FAA, and the airline will assign you to one of their bases.

Learn the Lingo

Here are a few words you're likely to hear as a flight attendant:

- **City codes** These are the abbreviations for the airports in U.S. and international cities. Most airlines require flight attendants to memorize at least several dozen airport codes, such as LAX (Los Angeles International Airport), DUB (Dublin), HKG (Hong Kong), and JFK (New York's John F. Kennedy Airport).

- **Hub** The city in which an airline is based and has its headquarters. Typically, this is where many transfer flights for a particular airline occur as well as flight attendant training.

- **Preflight briefing** This is the safety demonstration given to airline passengers before take-off. It often features a public address in which flight attendants show how to inflate an aircraft life vest.

See what it's like for flight attendants behind the scenes.

Finding a Job

Competition for flight attendant positions is always high, thanks to the great travel opportunities available to attendants. Airlines are looking for highly presentable and poised men and women who can interact comfortably with strangers and keep their cool in stressful situations. It's also important to be physically fit, as attendants are on their feet for most of the flight. A person's height also comes into play because attendants frequently have to reach into overhead bins and serve passengers hot liquids. Airlines also have vision requirements for flight attendants, although you are allowed to wear glasses or contacts.

Nowadays, most airlines will allow you to submit your résumé online, which greatly simplifies the process of applying for a position. With the exception of the interview, almost every part of the application process can be accomplished online. The interview is a crucial part of the process, so preparation is essential. Not only will your personality and customer service experience be assessed but your appearance and spoken manner are also important.

Tips for Success

- Never lose your patience! Being a flight attendant is both physically and mentally exhausting, but a good flight attendant will never let his or her exhaustion show. A sunny disposition is a secret to success in this business.

- Pay close attention to those around you. Things can turn from routine to urgent in very little time. Also keep a good rapport with your colleagues so that you work well together when things get stressful.

▲ **A flight attendant checks to see which passenger called for assistance.**

Reality Check

If flight attendants are not mindful, injuries can occur when opening overhead compartments or while pushing heavy service carts. In addition, flight attendants occasionally develop stress disorders from working long hours in a pressurized environment.

Related Jobs to Consider

Reservation ticket agent. Ticket agents also work for airlines and deal with nervous flyers. As a result, they receive customer service training similar to that of flight attendants.

Public-relations specialist. This job also requires you to have strong communication skills as well as a pulled-together appearance.

EMT. Like flight attendants, emergency medical technicians are safety professionals whose job it is to be calm even under trying circumstances.

LEARN MORE ONLINE

ASSOCIATION OF FLIGHT ATTENDANTS
The majority of flight attendants belong to this union. Their Web site teaches you a lot about what it means to be a flight attendant. http://www.afanet.org

THIRTY THOUSAND FEET
This is an informative gateway site that can link you to all kinds of information about the field, including some great job openings. http://www.thirtythousandfeet.com/flightat.htm

AIRLINE CAREER
This is another great Web site. Once you become a member, you can enroll in their flight attendant training program. http://airlinecareer.com

How to Move Up

- Like most jobs, putting in extra hours goes a long way in the airline industry. Most airlines guarantee a minimum of 65 to 85 flight hours per month, with the option to work additional hours. If you work hard and offer to work additional hours, not only will your superiors take notice but you'll also receive extra compensation for your time.

- After you have demonstrated that you are resourceful in crisis situations and capable of handling the job, you could be promoted to lead attendant, the highest attendant position aboard the aircraft. Lead attendants manage the other attendants aboard the aircraft and often take on additional responsibilities, such as recruiting and instructing other attendants.

- After working as a lead attendant, if you decide to move into another field, the experiences you've gathered as a flight attendant will prepare you for a host of other airline and non–airline-related jobs. Many flight attendants have gone on to become human resource managers, travel agents, public relations professionals, and airline consultants.

TEXT-DEPENDENT QUESTIONS

1. *What are fractional aircraft companies?*

2. *What is a typical day for a flight attendant?*

3. *About how many flight attendants are there in the United States?*

4. *How do you move up in this job?*

RESEARCH PROJECTS

1. *Explore life in the "friendly skies" by reading some memoirs from people who have done it, such as* Cruising Altitude *by Heather Poole,* Cockpit Confidential *by Patrick Smith, and* Skyfaring *by Mark Vanhoenacker.*

2. *Learn a new language. If you can take classes at school, that's great—but if not, there are some good apps that you can use on your own. Start learning for free with apps like Duolingo or busuu.*

Hotel Desk Clerk, Concierge, or Reservation Agent

Make guests' stays memorable. Meet interesting and diverse people. Be the face of your employer.

WORDS TO UNDERSTAND

irate: furious.
multitask: the ability to handle a few activities at the same time.
proficient: skillful.

Eloise, the famous children's book character who grew up at the Plaza Hotel, once said of hotel life that "getting bored is not allowed." Anyone who has ever worked at a hotel would probably agree with Eloise. When you're a desk clerk, concierge, or reservation agent, there's seldom a dull moment on the job. Your days are spent greeting guests and working out the details of their reservations, fulfilling their particular needs and desires, and advising them on where to go and what to see.

Hotels—which include resorts, extended-stay residences, and casinos—are located in every major town and city, as well as in far-flung spots of scenic beauty, which means that you could find work almost anywhere. Although high-end and high-volume establishments employ the greatest number of people, many smaller hotels and motels hire desk clerks with

◀ The desk clerk gives most guests their first impression of a hotel.

Although reservation agents work in offices where they're not on display, their jobs can be equally stressful. It is their responsibility to book rooms, quote rates, and answer any travel or scheduling questions that a guest may have. They spend a lot of time either talking to customers on the phone or answering e-mail inquiries about routes, schedules, rates, and types of accommodation. The job requires them to be **proficient** on the computer because reservation agents use proprietary networks to obtain information needed to make, change, or cancel reservations for customers.

In each of these positions—concierge, desk clerk, or reservation agent—work at times may feel like being in the midst of a traveling circus. However, beyond the day-to-day tasks, working in a hotel can be a fascinating experience. To fully appreciate the job, however, an employee must be willing to listen to and accommodate a diverse group of individuals, each with particular desires, attitudes, and even customs.

Who's Hiring?

- Commercial hotels
- Residential and extended-stay hotels
- Bed-and-breakfasts
- Inns
- Motels
- Resorts
- Casino hotels

Where Are the Jobs?

Most concierges and hotel reservation agents work for large chains because they have the highest volume of guests and reservations. Though the environment in a large hotel may not be as relaxed as at a smaller, family-run establishment, corporate-owned hotels and chains offer perks, such as discounts on travel rates, better benefits, and larger bonuses. Some corporate chains even help their employees further their education by assisting with the cost of hotel management coursework.

Although corporate hotels and chains technically employ more people, smaller hotels and motels with 10 or fewer employees still outnumber large ones. In these sorts of establishments, clerks often assume the responsibilities of both the concierge and the front desk manager. In addition to registering guests and answering the phones, clerks also bring fresh linens to rooms, handle the bookkeeping, and advise guests on places to visit. Although the responsibilities can be daunting at times, desk clerks have more autonomy at smaller establishments and may develop a better rapport with guests. Every type of establishment, however, has its share of demanding guests and stressful situations. For this reason, it's important for employees at these establishments to be levelheaded and patient.

▲ Although many reservations are made online, reservation agents are still important in the hotel industry, answering questions about rooms and accommodating special needs.

A Typical Day

Here are the highlights of a front desk clerk's day.

Arrive before the guests wake up. You usually arrive by 5 a.m. to check that wake-up calls and room-service orders are in place. Occasionally, you'll receive a call saying that a lightbulb went out in room 105 or that room 256 needs some aspirin, but usually the early mornings are the quietest time. You start going over the room assignments for the day.

Check them out. New guests typically start arriving after noon, which means that you need to have guests checked out and start the cleaning of the rooms well beforehand. If a guest hasn't checked out by 11:30, you give the room a call. In the midst of checking out, you'll also have to deal with your manager informing you of last-minute changes and requests.

Check them in. You review your registration list before everyone starts arriving. You see that Ms. Wiles, a favored guest, is checking in and make a note to address her by name. As guests arrive, you greet them warmly, and if you can tell from the reservation agent's notes

▲ A concierge helps guests choose what they need from the many activities and services offered by large hotels.

NOTES FROM THE FIELD

Front desk clerk, Los Angeles, California

Q: *How did you get your job?*

A: I applied for the job on Monster.com and received a response immediately. Several days later, I went in for an interview. The management was very laid-back, and the general feel of the place really appealed to me. I guess they thought I was a good fit for them as well because I was hired on the spot.

Q: *What do you like best about your job?*

A: As a child, I played secretary a lot, so—not surprisingly—I like filing, answering the phones, and problem solving. While I don't mind working in a people-oriented environment, the best part for me is being organized and handling administrative tasks.

Q: *What's the most challenging part of your job?*

A: Trying to please everyone is definitely the most challenging part of the job. You have to keep both the management and the guests happy, which can be difficult, particularly if you're dealing with a demanding guest.

Q: *What are the keys to success to being a front desk clerk?*

A: To be successful as a front desk agent you need to have patience. If you're organized and able to multitask, that will certainly help, but good communication is what matters most. If you're able to articulate your thoughts in a clear and eloquent fashion, you will go a long way in this business.

that a guest just flew in, ask them how their flight was. Most important, you get their credit card number and give them their room key and other pertinent information to help them get oriented and settled in their room.

Start Preparing Now

- Take classes in high school, such as speech, English, computers, and business that will give you an edge when working with customers or managing your other responsibilities.

- Check out the lodging management program that the Educational Institute of the American Hotel and Lodging Association (AHLA) offers to high school students.

- Research the lodging establishments in your area, and find out if any of the ones that interest you are looking for part-time employees.

Training and How to Get It

Experience carries almost as much weight as formal training in the hotel industry. Many hotels have a two-day orientation period, and if you are working as a front desk clerk or reservation agent, you don't need much more than that to get by. At an orientation, you will be introduced to your fellow employees and then given a detailed tour of every aspect of the hotel, from the emergency exits to the ice machine room. Hotel policies and regulations will also be explained during orientation. Many hotels and motels also have on-the-job training to supplement the orientation period. It is during this training period that desk clerks and reservation agents are taught how to use the computerized reservation and billing systems.

If you are seriously committed to working in the hotel industry, you might want to consider formal training. Upper management positions, such as general manager, hotel manager, food service manager, or sales manager typically require academic training in addition to on-the-job experience. Even if you don't desire a career as a manager, enrolling in a hotel management program or taking a class in this area is a good idea to keep in mind for the future. There are more than 800 schools across the United States that offer associate's degrees in hotel and restaurant management. Most of these programs provide students with both academic training and work experience in the various departments of a hotel.

If you do not have the time or the money for formal training, work on your customer service skills on your own. What matters most is that a desk clerk, reservation agent, or concierge is professional, likable, and uses good judgment. The rest can be taught.

Learn the Lingo

Here are a few words that you're likely to hear on the job:

- **Card entry** In lieu of a key, almost all hotels now use a card system to unlock hotel rooms. The entry card, which is about the size of a credit card, is set to work for however long a guest has paid to stay in the hotel.

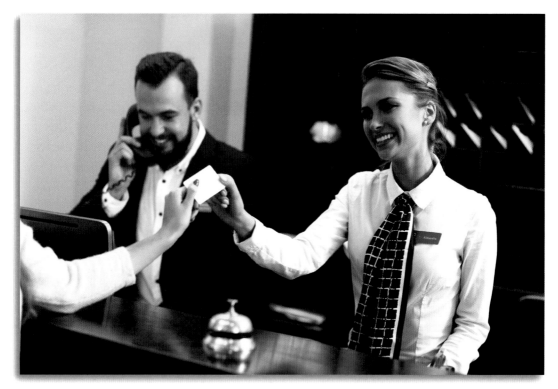

▲ A hotel desk clerk must be efficient and organized, but a welcoming smile is just as important.

- **Honesty bar** This is hotel-speak for an unattended beverage bar in the lobby or lounge of a hotel, where payment is left to the patron. By contrast, anything taken from a room minibar is automatically charged to the guest's account.

- **HVAC** This acronym, which stands for "heating, ventilation, and air conditioning," is frequently used to describe the hotel's climate control system.

Finding a Job

Many small or independently run hotels hire high school workers as part-time desk clerks, so if you are willing to work at night or during holiday periods, a front office job can serve as a great stepping-stone to a full-time job. The best way to land an entry-level hotel job—be it a full- or part-time position—is to find a hotel or motel that interests you, introduce yourself to the manager, and ask him or her if there are any job openings available. This sort of friendly and direct approach is just what hotel managers are looking for in an employee. Remember, though, to dress as professionally as the job would require.

Tips for Success

- Project your best self. Apart from having a winning personality, being detail oriented can really make a difference. Skills like good spelling and a clear speaking voice can really make a difference.

- *Parlez-vous francais*? Because many hotels attract an international clientele, speaking a foreign language can be very helpful, particularly at high-end hotels and resorts.

Reality Check

Automated check-in and checkout procedures reduce the backlog of guests waiting for desk service and may reduce peak front-desk staffing needs in many establishments. Nevertheless, the front desk remains the principal point of contact for guests at most properties. Backlogs at busy checkout times can happen quickly, and guests needing to make flights can get quite **irate**.

LEARN MORE ONLINE

AMERICAN HOTEL AND LODGING ASSOCIATION
This professional association is a leading organization in the hospitality field and provides much useful information on its Web site for people interested in learning more about a career as a lodging professional. http://www.ahla.com

HCAREERS
This is a jobs board and research site presented by the hospitality industry and includes many useful links for people wanting to learn more about the scope of opportunities. http://www.hcareers.com

Related Jobs to Consider

Real estate agent. As with the work of reservation agents, this job entails a lot of social talking with clients and prospective customers—here, to sell or rent an apartment or house.

Restaurant host or hostess. Restaurants and hotels can have the same frenetic pace and energy. To work in either, employees must have patience and stamina. In addition, they need impeccable customer service skills.

See what it's like to be a concierge.

How to Move Up

- Just as many Hollywood executives began their careers in studio mailrooms, many hotel owners started as bellhops and worked their way up. Front office jobs at hotels can serve as a great stepping-stone to management positions.

- After a few years of working the desk, clerks are typically rewarded with promotions. Though it is often easier to find work at a small inn or motel, large hotel and motel chains have greater advancement opportunities.

- Chain hotels and motels also typically have programs designed to help employees set and achieve career goals. Large hotels and chains also have management training programs, in which desk clerks and concierges are sometimes asked to participate.

TEXT-DEPENDENT QUESTIONS

1. *What does a concierge do?*
2. *About how many hotel desk clerks are there in the United States?*
3. *How do you look for a job in this field?*
4. *How might you move up in this field?*

RESEARCH PROJECTS

1. *There are nearly as many types of hotels as there are types of travelers. Research the different kinds and try to figure out what sort of lodging establishment would best suit your personality. For example, could you picture yourself in a glitzy casino hotel? Or a quaint bed-and-breakfast?*

2. *Research training programs offered through Educational Institute of the American Hotel and Lodging Association (AHLA). They have initiated lodging management programs in hundreds of high schools in the United States. Their two-year program for juniors and seniors teaches management principles and leads to a professional certification. (See https://www.ahlei.org/Programs/High-School-Program-(HTMP)/)*

Cook/Food-Prep Worker

Create new and exciting dishes. Bask in the glory of a satisfied customer's smile. Work in a dynamic environment.

WORDS TO UNDERSTAND

chaotic: extremely busy, even disorderly.

diligent: hard-working.

executive chef: the top chef in a kitchen, who plans the menus and supervises the kitchen staff.

A generation ago, dining out was reserved for dates and special occasions; nowadays it's a way of life. The rise in two-income households and the number of busy, overcommitted adults has created a boom in the restaurant industry. Americans now spend nearly half their food budget in restaurants, which is one reason the restaurant industry is so busy. Of course, being a chef is by no means as easy as Rachel Ray or the Food Network makes it look. The hours are long, the work is physically demanding, and the atmosphere can be high pressure, but the thrill of watching your smiling customers savoring one of your meals makes it worth the while.

◀ A restaurant may appear to be calm in the dining room, but the kitchen is always hectic. Chefs work hard under pressure to deliver great tasting food and a beautiful presentation.

Is This Job Right for You?

Answer the following questions to see whether a career in cooking or food prep is right for you.

Yes	No	
Yes	No	1. *Can you handle a fast-paced environment?*
Yes	No	2. *Do you have a love of food?*
Yes	No	3. *Do you enjoy cooking for others?*
Yes	No	4. *Are you safety-minded and responsible?*
Yes	No	5. *Do you work well in stressful situations?*
Yes	No	6. *Are you in good shape and able to lift heavy pots and pans?*
Yes	No	7. *Do you have strong teamwork skills?*
Yes	No	8. *Can you be on your feet for hours?*
Yes	No	9. *Are you interested in cooking techniques and principles?*
Yes	No	10. *Do you have a sharp sense of taste and smell?*

If you answered "Yes" to most or all of these questions, you should consider a career as a cook. To find out more about this job, read on.

What's the Work Like?

A cook's job varies, depending on the position in the kitchen and the type of dining establishment. This said, all cooks are responsible for creating and preparing dishes under tight time pressures. If you are working in a large restaurant, you and your fellow kitchen workers may have to prepare dozens of meals in a few hours. To accomplish such an overwhelming undertaking, you must be physically fit and able to work well with others. Cooking in a professional kitchen is comparable to a team sport; if one player is down, the rest of the team suffers. While becoming an **executive chef** at an upscale restaurant requires extensive training and experience, there

TALKING MONEY

The median hourly earnings for a restaurant cook are $12.23, but the pay varies depending on the type and location of the establishment and specific job duties. For example, a fast-food cook typically earns $9.89 an hour, according to the U.S. Bureau of Labor Statistics, whereas a prep worker earns $10.31. But private chefs earn an average of $20.30 per hour.

are plenty of kitchen jobs available to those with little or no training. Here is a brief introduction to some of the kitchen players:

- Food preparation workers are in charge of prepping the food. They chop the vegetables, trim the meats, stir the sauces, and keep the work areas clean.

- Line cooks (also called assistant cooks) manage a specific station. Their title usually indicates what they cook. For example, the fry cook manages the frying station.

- Short-order cooks work in establishments that emphasize quick service, such as coffee shops, diners, or lunch counters. They handle multiple orders at the same time and are the ones grilling burgers, frying eggs, and cooking french fries simultaneously.

▲ Line cooks prep ingredients for the evening rush.

Who's Hiring?

- Full-service restaurants

- Coffee shops and diners

- Cafeterias in hospitals, schools, and corporations

- Limited dining establishments in park and recreation centers

- Resort, hotel, and casino dining establishments, which may offer seasonal employment

- Catering companies and banquet halls, which may also operate on a seasonal or part-time basis

Watch line cooks at work.

▲ **A short-order cook prepares sandwiches on the griddle at a diner.**

Where Are the Jobs?

Insiders say one of the perks of being a cook is that you can find employment just about anywhere. Though the best-paid jobs tend to be located in big cities and high-end resort areas, today there are thousands of restaurants in every state and at least one in every town. In other words, expertise as a cook is great to have if you like to travel and want to be mobile.

TALKING TRENDS

The restaurant industry currently employs an estimated 14.7 million people, and according to the U.S. Bureau of Labor Statistics, it will continue to add jobs over the next decade. The number of food preparation jobs is expected to keep pace with the rest of the economy.

The shift you take—morning, afternoon, or evening—will greatly affect your duties. If you work in a coffee shop or a local restaurant that attracts the lunch crowd, the morning and afternoon shifts are typically the most **chaotic**. Everyone wants to eat quickly and get back to work, so orders will be flying at you right and left. Although the morning and afternoon shifts are often the most chaotic kitchen environment, the good news is that your day is usually over by 4 or 5 p.m. On the contrary, upscale restaurants or restaurants with large bars usually attract the dinner crowd. Cooks on the evening shift usually work until midnight or later, and as a result, they are usually paid more money.

Working nights at a popular restaurant can be extremely trying. The hours are long, and the dishes are more elaborate to prepare; however, if you want to climb the culinary ladder, working the night shift will put more money in your pocket and demonstrate that you are a hard worker.

A Typical Day

Here are the highlights of a typical day in the kitchen of a small restaurant.

Get started. When you first walk in, you turn on the ovens. If everything looks in order, you head to the refrigerator and examine your food supply. Let's say you have a lot of cabbage left over from the day before, you'll probably want to add a cabbage soup to "Today's Specials."

Begin prep. After the menu and today's specials have been decided, it's time to start preparing the foods. This is largely the prep workers' job, but everyone lends a hand. Vegetables are sliced, soups and sauces are made ahead of time, and meats are thawed and prepared for cooking.

NOTES FROM THE FIELD

Head cook, *Los Angeles, California*

Q: *How did you get your job?*

A: My aunt had a restaurant, and as a kid in Louisiana, I always liked to hang out in it. When I moved to Los Angeles, I started working as an assistant cook at the Cozy Corner in downtown L.A. Once the head cook left, I took over for him. That restaurant eventually closed, so I came here as head cook. When I first started, we just had counter seating, but over the years we've expanded to become a 65-seat restaurant.

Q: *What do you like best about your job?*

A: Seeing a smile on a customer's face when they get up from one of our meals. I also like to create new dishes, but mostly I like making our customers happy. It's very flattering when someone from as far away as New York passes by fancier restaurants to come to our café. We put out quality food, and I'm proud of that.

Q: *What's the most challenging part of your job?*

A: The hours. I get up almost every day at 4 in the morning to bake the pies, roast the turkeys, and prepare the soups and sauces. We cook all of our meals on the premises, and all of our ingredients are fresh, so it takes a lot of time and effort.

Q: *What are the keys to success to being a cook?*

A: Being consistent. If your quality of food is consistent, in time you will develop a loyal following. I try to treat every customer like a family member. Restaurants thrive on word of mouth, so if you make a mistake, you're probably losing more than just one customer.

Get into high gear. Once customers start arriving, the kitchen kicks into high gear. You are simultaneously grilling burgers, poaching eggs, and, perhaps, filleting salmon. Depending on where you work and how busy it is, you may have to prepare 50 or more orders in a few hours. Time becomes a blur. Then once your shift starts to wind down, you're almost wiped out.

Start Preparing Now

- Look for a vocational-education course or program in culinary careers at your high school.

- Try to find a part-time job or internship at a local restaurant or coffee shop.

- Learn about and experiment with food. Cooking is supposed to be fun, so try to cook as much as possible for your family, friends, and coworkers.

Training and How to Get It

Above all else, what you'll need to succeed in the culinary world is a strong work ethic coupled with a lot of on-the-job experience. Paying your dues, so to speak, is an integral part of becoming a good chef. Many of the celebrity chefs that you see on television initially began as short-order cooks or prep-workers. Emeril Lagasse started as a baker in a small Portuguese bakery in Massachusetts, and today he has multiple restaurants and cookbooks to his name. While a fancy culinary degree can get your foot in the door, if you demonstrate leadership skills and an eagerness to learn new cooking techniques, you might move up fast in the culinary world.

If you have the time, summer internships or part-time jobs are both great ways to break into the culinary field. Even if you have zero experience in the kitchen, chances are good that you can find work as a food-prep worker. The job requires little training, and you'll be able to see firsthand how a kitchen is run. For high school students, vocational schools usually offer culinary courses that prepare students for work as a short-order cook at a diner or a cook's assistant at a fancy restaurant. Most courses begin with kitchen sanitation and go on to teach basic training in preparing food, such as slicing and dicing methods for meats and vegetables, as well as basic cooking methods, such as baking, broiling, and grilling. Although internships and cooking classes will help you land a job, don't underestimate the training that can be found in your own kitchen. If you experiment with food and cook as much as possible for your family, friends, and coworkers, you'll eventually develop your own cooking style—something that is hard to accomplish when you are working at a restaurant or in the middle of an instructed class.

Learn the Lingo

Here are a few words you'll hear in a commercial kitchen:

- **Blanche** To plunge into boiling liquid and cook to 10 to 20 percent of doneness.

- **Choice grade** The second-highest USDA quality grade for meat, indicating good-brittle fat, good marbling, and good-textured flesh; the most commonly used grade of meat.

- **Cost control** The practice of ensuring that food costs are managed so that they stay within a set range and so the business can earn a profit.

- **Slack time** Kitchen jargon referring to time allowed for a product to undergo a change—a frozen product to thaw, juices in cooked meats to settle, dough to rest in baking.

- **Sous-chef** This French word means, literally, "under-chef." Sous-chefs are skilled cooks working in large or upscale restaurants who work underneath the executive chef. They often supervise the various cooking stations.

- **Partial cooking** Any cooking process that is stopped before the product is fully cooked, and then refrigerated until needed, at which point it is fully cooked. This process is often used for large-quantity or commercial cooking.

Finding a Job

The restaurant industry is the largest employer in the United States outside of the government, so those working in the restaurant business are not likely to go hungry any time soon. There are dozens of culinary-related jobs listed online or in your local newspaper. For those working in a major metropolis, Craigslist.org can be a great resource. It's not hard to find a job in this field; however, if you are looking to work in an upscale dining establishment, you'll probably need to network a bit.

If you don't know anyone in the restaurant industry, you can always join an association, such as the National Restaurant Association (NRA). For a small membership fee, associations such as the NRA can put you in touch with top chefs in your area. Persistence is the key to finding a job in the restaurant industry. Because restaurants have such a high turnover rate, jobs go fast. When you see a position that you like, act quickly. A hard worker is the most valuable asset to have in the kitchen, so if you don't have the experience necessary, be sure to stress that you are a **diligent** and dependable person.

Tips for Success

- Culinary passion and the ability to work well with others are the two most essential ingredients to becoming a good chef. That said, it is equally important to be an organized and dependable worker.

- Be clean and look clean. Foodborne illness is commonly spread by poor hygiene, especially the failure to wash hands. For this reason most establishments will want to avoid even the appearance of uncleanliness and will want every worker to reflect a regard for good practices.

- Learning Spanish is a good idea. A lot of kitchen staff, especially in cities, speak it as a first language.

Reality Check

The top culinary schools can be as pricey as private colleges, but the wages of chefs and cooks in many parts of the United States aren't on par. Figure out the cooking salaries in your area if you're tempted to take out a hefty loan for culinary school, so you know whether you can pay it back.

▲ Culinary school can be a good way to get a leg up in the industry. But before taking out a large student loan, figure out if the salaries in your area will allow you to pay it back.

Related Jobs to Consider

Caterer. If you are a social person, who likes cooking but doesn't want to be in the kitchen all day, you might want to consider the catering field.

Maitre d' or hostess. For those who like the atmosphere and vibe of a restaurant, but don't want to get their hands dirty, consider this often well-paid alternative.

Nutritionist. This is a great job for people who live a healthy lifestyle and think that food is the most essential ingredient to a long and happy life.

LEARN MORE ONLINE

THE NATIONAL RESTAURANT ASSOCIATION
This is the leading business association for the restaurant industry. Their web site offers up-to-date industry facts as well as information on where to find jobs. http://www.restaurant.org

STAR CHEFS
A magazine for culinary experts as well as those interested in learning about the culinary industry. It's also a great place to find a job or post your résumé. http://www.starchefs.com

How to Move Up

- Put in the extra effort. The restaurant industry doesn't operate on a normal 9-to-5 basis. Putting in long hours and offering to take on more responsibility in the kitchen will go a long way.

- Become an expert in a specific culinary field. Specializing in a certain cuisine or type of food, such as desserts or Asian cuisine, can really set you apart from the rest.

- Focus on management. Volunteer to help out with administrative tasks, such as food ordering and staffing, to help yourself become more valuable.

TEXT-DEPENDENT QUESTIONS

1. *What are some of the different places cooks work?*

2. *What's one of the better-paying cook jobs? One of the lower-paying?*

3. *What kind of training do you need for these jobs?*

4. *How might you go about looking for work in this field?*

RESEARCH PROJECTS

1. *Try your hand at creating a whole meal for a group of family and friends. Plan appetizers, main dishes and salads, and dessert. Take charge of the shopping, the prep work, and service—and don't forget the cleanup, which is an important part of this job, too!*

2. *Explore cooking techniques you've never tried before. For instance, check out the how-to videos on epicurious.com, or look for instructional books from the America's Test Kitchen series.*

▲ Take cooking classes and practice by preparing meals for family and friends.

Waiter, Waitress, Host, or Hostess

Work with a diverse group of people. Create your own working hours. Put a smile on a customer's face.

WORDS TO UNDERSTAND

front-of-house: here, describes restaurant workers who deal directly with the customers, such as wait staff and hosts.

multitask: to handle multiple activities at the same time.

placate: to pacify or soothe someone.

Wait staff and hosts are the ambassadors of the kitchen. If something is wrong with a meal, it's not the chef who will hear from the customers, it's the food servers. A good waitress or waiter makes customers feel like they are the only ones in the room. He or she is attentive, but not intrusive. During busy hours, when there are 30 tables of customers waiting for food, servers must be able to **multitask** with smiles on their faces. In addition to memorizing specials, taking customers' orders, and ringing up a check, food servers must also keep their cool, even when they have a rude patron and seven other tables to serve. Similarly, hosts or hostesses greet and seat customers while tracking what the waitstaff is doing and keep waiting customers happy. If you're friendly, fast on your feet, and good at multitasking, you might consider becoming one of the millions of **front-of-house** staffers in the United States.

◀ In addition to keeping track of who's ordered what, waitstaff must remember menu specials and satisfy patrons' expectations.

Is This Job Right for You?

Would being a waiter, waitress, host, or hostess be right for you? To find out, read each of the following statements and answer "Yes" or "No."

Yes	No		
Yes	No	1.	*Are you friendly and patient?*
Yes	No	2.	*Do you like helping others?*
Yes	No	3.	*Can you keep your cool in stressful situations?*
Yes	No	4.	*Can you work on your feet for long periods?*
Yes	No	5.	*Are you good at basic arithmetic?*
Yes	No	6.	*Can you anticipate others' needs?*
Yes	No	7.	*Can you keep a professional manner?*
Yes	No	8.	*Would you be willing to work weekends and holidays?*
Yes	No	9.	*Do you like the hustle and bustle of restaurants?*
Yes	No	10.	*Do you have a good memory for specials and orders?*

If you answered "Yes" to most of these questions, consider a career as a waiter, waitress, host, or hostess. To find out more about these positions, read on.

What's the Work Like?

As a waiter or waitress, your primary responsibility would be to take orders, serve food and beverages, and ensure that the check is accurate and arrives in a timely manner. While these may seem like simple tasks, a shocking amount of sweat and savvy goes into creating a pleasant dining experience. Not only are waiters and waitresses on their feet all day long, they typically carry heavy trays of food-laden dishes. They also must be able to work efficiently. Waiters and waitresses face heavy pressure to serve customers quickly, especially during busy dining periods. Waitresses or waiters who get behind in their orders or mix their orders up can quickly come under fire from belligerent diners. Waitresses and

TALKING MONEY

The median hourly earnings (including tips) of wait staff was $9.61 per hour, but the rates vary widely; the highest-paid workers earn more than twice that average. Meanwhile, hosts and hostesses tend to average more at $10.29 an hour, according to 2016 data from the U.S. Bureau of Labor Statistics.

waiters must charm the customer in an unobtrusive way, making sure all of the customer's needs are met, and when something goes wrong in the kitchen—an order is dropped or the steak is overdone—it is the waiter or waitress who must **placate** the customer and deal with the fallout.

A host's or hostess' primary responsibility is to seat customers in a courteous manner, handing them menus, and escorting them to their tables. Another important part of the job involves caring for the waitstaff and making sure that they are working efficiently. In addition to all this, hosts and hostesses also have to answer the phones, and in most cases, book reservations. If you work in a busy restaurant, this can be the most difficult part of the job. On a busy night, you'll be running around to seat customers, check on the waitstaff to see how the tables are moving, and deal with a menu question or seating problem. Also, depending on the restaurant, you'll have to reserve tables for the following week amidst all the restaurant chaos.

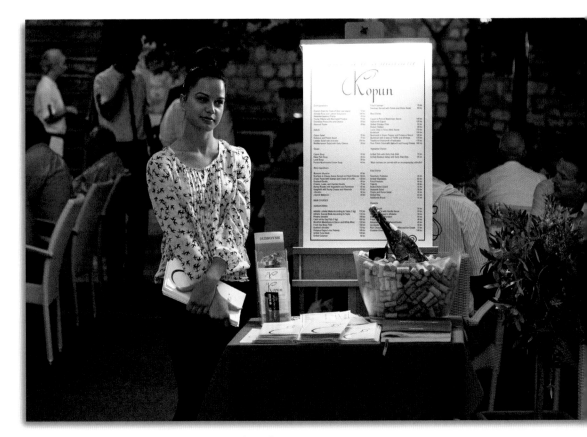

▲ **A hostess stands ready to greet restaurant patrons.**

Who's Hiring?

- Full-service restaurants

- Hotels, resorts, casinos, and cruise ships

- Amusement parks and certain other recreational facilities

- Corporate cafeterias

- Coffee shops and diners

- Banquet halls

- Assisted living facilities

Where Are the Jobs?

Unlike hosts or hostesses, who typically work at upscale restaurants, a job waiting tables can vary greatly depending on the size and type of establishment. In coffee shops, where straight-forward dishes are prepared, fast and efficient service is the most important aspect of the job. In top restaurants where the meals are prepared to order, the emphasis is on customer care. It's important to remember that at a good restaurant the customer is paying for more than just a tasty meal: They're also paying for high-quality service. Waiters and waitresses need to be able to recommend certain dishes and identify ingredients, or explain how various items on the menu are prepared. In some places, a waiter may even be called on to light a flambé at the table.

The shift a waitress or waiter works—morning, afternoon, or evening—will also affect the job environment. Morning and afternoon shifts at local restaurants and coffee shops tend to be the busiest because they typically serve work crowds, most of whom want to eat quickly and without much fanfare. It's an exhausting shift, but the upside is getting all evening off to recover. By contrast, the evening shift tends to be the most stressful at upscale or popular restaurants. Diners are paying more for their meals, and in turn, they expect better service.

TALKING TRENDS

These days, dining out is a national pastime. This adds up to more than 2.6 million waiting jobs in the United States, and 400,000 hosting jobs. Forecasters predict steady growth in the demand for people to fill all these jobs, especially as the baby boom generation retires and has more time to eat out.

▲ Remember, good service is as important as the food. A friendly and helpful attitude means happy patrons and better tips.

Although you may initially be less interested in working a busy or stressful shift, keep in mind that you'll make substantially more money in tips during the busy hours.

A Typical Day

Here are the highlights of a typical evening shift at a restaurant.

Set up before dinner. Arrive at 4 p.m. and check in with the host or hostess. If there is a birthday party or special event that evening, you'll probably need to coordinate with the host and help with setup.

Serve the meals. You speed from table to table, taking orders, serving food and drinks, and making sure that the food is prepared well and the customers are satisfied.

Deliver the check! Once coffee and deserts have been offered or ordered, it's time to compute the check. It's your job to make sure that everything ordered is accounted for, and that customers receive their checks in a timely manner. Once your last customer's check is closed out, and you've talked with the host or hostess, you've finished your shift.

▲ Waiters and waitresses must learn to maneuver through busy restaurants with multiple meals to serve.

Start Preparing Now

- Do some research on dining establishments in your area, and decide what sort of restaurant or establishment interests you most.

- Learn by doing: get a part-time or weekend job in a restaurant.

- Have lunch or dinner at the dining establishments that interest you and introduce yourself to the manager or owner.

Training and How to Get It

One of the best parts about being a waiter or waitress is that there is always an abundance of positions at your disposal, and most of them don't need formal training. At high-end restaurants, previous restaurant experience is often a requirement, but for the most part, the training you'll need can be acquired on the job. Although previous restaurant experience gives you a major edge, the most important point to finding work as a waiter or waitress is to

NOTES FROM THE FIELD

Hostess, Madison, Wisconsin

Q: *How did you get your job?*

A: My timing was perfect, though I didn't know it at the time. I just waltzed through the door of L'Etoile restaurant with a thoughtful cover letter and my résumé. You have to take a chance. I believe I got the job because I was motivated, interested, and insisted on hand-delivering my résumé to the mâitre d'. That way I could have an impromptu interview and really sell myself. I told him that I would work hard and that I had immense respect for the restaurant, and eventually he offered me the job.

Q: *What do you like best about your job?*

A: I like manning the ship. The host stands at the helm of the restaurant and is responsible for getting everyone moving. I like thinking on my feet, solving problems as they arise, interacting with different people, and anticipating the needs of both the patrons and the team around me.

Q: *What's the most challenging part of the job?*

A: Difficult people can be quite challenging. The skill lies in a host's ability to exercise patience, be sympathetic, and diffuse escalating situations that can arise when patrons have to wait for a table or are discontented with the service. Of course the secret to being really good at this job is to think ahead. That way you avoid the possibility of angry or dissatisfied patrons.

Q: *What are the keys to success to being a host or hostess?*

A: Be real. No one wants to contend with a phony hostess who speaks in circles. It's always better to be straightforward with patrons because they can usually tell if you're lying. It's also important to show respect to the kitchen, the servers, the bartenders, and the dishwashers. Finally, you need to take initiative in every aspect of the job. Make yourself an asset to the team.

project a personable and professional vibe. Good waiters or waitresses are often good sales-people. Convincing the customer to order that expensive wine at the beginning of the meal and have that desert and coffee at the end makes employers happy and brings in bigger tips, so previous sales experience or experience working with customers in other positions can be a major plus.

Landing a job as a host or hostess is often more challenging and generally requires previous kitchen or waiting experience. However there are plenty of service industry jobs that will prepare you for the many logistical challenges that hosts and hostesses must deal with on a daily basis. For instance, hotel, resort, or casino jobs, such as front desk manager positions, provide comparable training.

Learn the Lingo

Here are a few words you'll hear as a waiter, waitress, host, or hostess:

- **Back of the house** The kitchen and storage areas where the chefs, cooks, prep people, and dishwashers primarily work.

- **Double** Two shifts in a row: "I'm exhausted, I just pulled a double."

- **Push a dish** When you have a surplus of a certain ingredient or dish, the kitchen will often tell servers to recommend it—"Push the Cajun catfish—it won't be good tomorrow!"

- **Stiffed** Describes a server whose customer leaves without tipping.

Finding a Job

Because the restaurant industry has such a fast turnover rate, positions waiting tables open regularly. If you come across as responsible, friendly, presentable, and quick-minded, you have a good chance of finding a job as a waiter or waitress. The most effective strategy is simply to walk into a dozen or so restaurants in your neighborhood and introduce yourself to the manager; chances are you'll find at least one place that is looking for a new waiter or waitress. If this method sounds unappealing, however, there are Web sites, such as Craigslist.org and Monster.com, that offer a venue for job listings, as do a few associations, such as the American Hotel and Lodging Association, http://www.ahla.com

Once you've gained some experience, you may be able to move to a restaurant where there's a likelihood of a promotion to a position such as headwaiter or host or hostess. Restaurant managers are also often recruited from the ranks of experienced and competent waitstaff.

Tips for Success

- Offer a smile! Friendliness is next to godliness in the service industry, so be sure to smile and be welcoming.

- Don't waste time. Efficiency is also key to succeeding in this business. It won't matter how nice you are if it takes you forever to serve drinks or ring up the check. Slow or forgetful waiters or waitresses can sacrifice their tips.

 Watch a training video for wait staff.

▲ Dealing with unhappy patrons is part of the job even when it's not your fault.

Reality Check

Though there is never a lack of food service jobs available, competition can be stiff, particularly in large cities. Job openings are often snatched up quickly by actors and other creative types attracted to the flexible hours. It's also important to remember that a lot of restaurants are looking for part-time workers, which isn't suitable for everyone. According to the Bureau of Labor Statistics, nearly half of the Americans who worked part-time jobs in 2004 were waiters and waitresses.

LEARN MORE ONLINE

NATIONAL RESTAURANT ASSOCIATION
This is the leading association for the restaurant industry. Their Web site offers up-to-date industry facts as well as information on where to find jobs. http://www.restaurant.org

INTERNATIONAL COUNCIL ON HOTEL, RESTAURANT, AND INSTITUTIONAL EDUCATION
One great way to better understand and appreciate the restaurant industry on an international level is to browse this Web site. It also offers tips on finding jobs. http://www.chrie.org

Related Jobs to Consider

Retail Sales Assistant. As with waiting tables, a large part of retail involves serving customers and handling money. Friendliness, efficiency, and sharp social skills are prized skills in both professions.

Caterer. Caterers work with food in social settings, which is similar to waiting tables or hostessing. The job also comes with a flexible schedule. However, caterers tend to work out of an office and spend a lot more time with their customers.

How to Move Up

- Put in those extra hours. The restaurant industry prides itself on being fast paced and stress inducing, so those who work hard and take on the double shift are often rewarded.

- Show an interest in your customers and your coworkers. Restaurants, more so than many other businesses, are run like families, so it's important to show you care about the food and how the establishment is being run. If you like a certain dish, let the kitchen and management know. Little things like this demonstrate a commitment and show that you are part of the team.

- Take a class. If you're invested in becoming a restaurant manager or owner one day, you'll want to take at least one class in food service management and accounting. Alternatively, you might want to consider taking some culinary courses.

TEXT-DEPENDENT QUESTIONS

1. *What's the difference between "front of house" and "back of house"?*

2. *About how many waiters and waitresses are there in the United States?*

3. *What kind of training do you need for these jobs?*

4. *What are some ways to move up in this field?*

RESEARCH PROJECTS

1. *Try out waiting tables and see if you like it. If you can't find part-time or seasonal work, you might want to try a catering company in your area. The summer and holiday season are the busiest times of year for catering companies, so caterers are always looking for high school or college students to fill in during these times.*

2. *Because wait staffers depend on tips, there is lots of advice out there about how to maximize your income. Check out books like* **The Ultimate Waiter** *by Robert McHalffey,* **the Renegade Server** *by Tim Kirkland, and* **How to Increase Your Tips** *by Riccardo Sanchez.*

Is This Job Right for You?

To find out if being a bartender is right for you, read each of the following statements and answer "Yes" or "No."

Yes	No		
Yes	No	**1.**	*Do you enjoy talking to a wide variety of people?*
Yes	No	**2.**	*Are you a fast and effective worker?*
Yes	No	**3.**	*Can you work in noisy environments?*
Yes	No	**4.**	*Do you have a good memory for drink proportions and names?*
Yes	No	**5.**	*Are you friendly and a good listener?*
Yes	No	**6.**	*Are you comfortable working late at night?*
Yes	No	**7.**	*Can you work on your feet for hours at a time?*
Yes	No	**8.**	*Are you assertive and able to deal with unruly customers?*
Yes	No	**9.**	*Are you trustworthy and able to handle money efficiently?*
Yes	No	**10.**	*Would you be able to resist drinking on the job?*

If you answered "Yes" to most of the questions, you may have what it takes to be a bartender. To find out more about this profession, read on.

What's the Work Like?

As a bartender, your main job is to fill drink orders either from customers at the bar or from waiters and waitresses delivering drinks to seated customers. Though this may sound routine, a surprising amount of focus and energy goes into preparing a well-mixed drink. From Singapore slings and sidecars to mud slides and martinis, you must know a wide range of drink recipes—and be able to mix them exactly. You may even create your own house specialty drinks. In addition to being fast, knowledgeable, and friendly, bartenders have a surprising amount of responsibility. They must keep tabs

TALKING MONEY

Bartenders earn a median hourly wage of $10.00 per hour, or about $28,800 a year, according to 2016 data from the U.S. Bureau of Labor Statistics. Gratuities can boost a bartender's income significantly: bartenders working in swanky metropolitan bars frequented by big tippers can earn as much as $60 an hour. Like waiters and waitresses, bartenders may receive more than half of their earnings as tips.

▲ To be on the safe side of the law, a bartender should ask for proof of age from anyone who looks under 25.

on how much everyone has been drinking, particularly if a person is alone or appears to be the designated driver. Bartenders must also check the identification of customers seated at the bar. Even though the legal drinking age in the United States is 21, bartenders should ask for identification from anyone who looks under the age of 25.

Drinks aside, there are a host of smaller tasks that bartenders manage. These include collecting money from customers seated at the bar, operating the cash register, and ordering and maintaining an inventory of liquors. In addition, you may be asked to wash glassware and utensils or serve food to customers seated at the bar.

Who's Hiring?

- Full-service and family-owned restaurants

- Traditional bars and pubs

- Large-scale clubs or lounges

- Hotels, resorts, casinos, and cruise ships

- Sports arenas and certain other recreational facilities

- Banquet halls

- Caterers

Where Are the Jobs?

The majority of bartenders work behind a bar, where they serve and interact with patrons. This job requires you to be **gregarious** and talkative, particularly if you want a good tip. Bartenders at service bars, on the other hand, have far less contact with customers. Service bars are usually small in size and located in the corners of restaurants, hotels, and clubs. Generally speaking, it's a place where waiters and waitresses place drink orders.

At large bars and clubs with high occupancy levels, some bartenders use equipment that automatically measures, pours, and mixes drinks at the push of a button, such as a margarita mixer. Bartenders who work in large bars may not do as much mixing, but they still must work quickly to handle a large volume of drink orders and be familiar with the ingredients for special drink requests. Regardless of where a bartender works, he or she will still have to fill drink orders by hand.

TALKING TRENDS

Today there are about 611,200 bartenders serving drinks in the United States, and job growth overall will depend on the type of venue. Full-service restaurants are expected to expand as increasing numbers of people eat out more frequently. Bartending jobs at these establishments are expected to increase. On the other hand, the Bureau of Labor Statistics forecasts that the number of bars and pubs will decrease in number through 2024.

▲ Working at a large bar or club is different than working at the local pub. There may be a large crowd and loud music, but the tips could be better too.

A Typical Day

Here are typical highlights for a bartender working an evening shift.

Get in the saddle. You arrive at about 4 p.m. Since most people are at work at this hour, you ease into your shift by wiping down the bar, preparing margarita and mai tai mix, and making sure that there are enough clean glasses for the evening.

Make that one happy-but-hectic hour. Happy hour or no happy hour, the busiest time for many bartenders is between 6 and 8 p.m. when the after-work crowd arrives. You may be taking up to five orders a minute, which can be overwhelming. On top of that, you'll have to keep track of multiple tabs and make sure that no one has had too much to drink.

Close out or burn the midnight oil. Depending on your establishment's hours and clientele, either your customers will start to clear out by 10 p.m. or things may become **chaotic**. If you work in a restaurant bar, the crowd will start to wind down, and after washing some dishes, wiping down the bar, and doing some bottle inventory, you'll be able to leave. If you work at a late-night establishment, 1 to 2 a.m. will probably be your busiest hour.

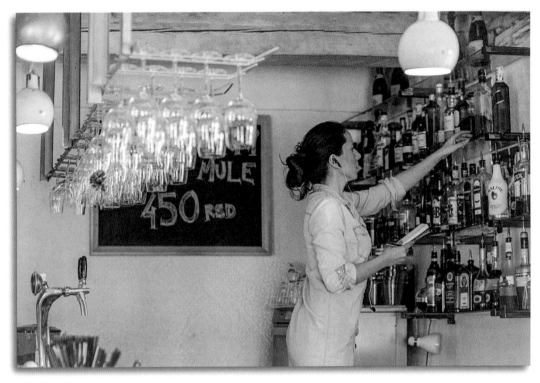

▲ Before the bar opens for business, the bartender takes inventory of what is in stock.

Start Preparing Now

• If you're between 18 and 21 years of age, check to see what your state's minimum age is to work as a bartender. Usually, bartenders must be at least 21, but in some states, you can start as early as 18. If you're of age, you should try finding part-time or seasonal work as a bartender.

• Catering companies can provide you with valuable experience. The summer and holiday season are the busiest times of year for catering companies, so caterers are always looking for high school or college students to fill in during these times.

Training and How to Get It

Although some employers require you to have specialized training in food handling, most bartenders face no degree requirements for their job (although in some states they do face age requirements). Employers are more likely to hire and promote based on people skills and personal qualities rather than on education. The most important training for bartending is practice.

NOTES FROM THE FIELD

Bartender, *Los Angeles, California*

Q: *How did you get your job?*

A: The owner of Birds is a friend of mine. We used to tend bar side by side. When she and her husband told me that they were planning on opening a bar of their own, I said, "Let me know when that happens, and I'll come work for you." Two years later, they called to tell me that they'd bought a place. Every job I've landed was the result of knowing someone at that particular bar.

Q: *What do you like best about your job?*

A: I like that I can make a very comfortable living from a part-time job, and I don't "bring my work home with me." I'm also fortunate to work at Birds. Not every bar offers the earning potential of a recognized Hollywood tourist stop, but even a little neighborhood spot can offer a decent level of income.

Q: *What's the most challenging part of your job?*

A: The alcohol. It can be one of the most insidious substances on the planet. Dealing with it, and the consumers of it, can be both spiritually taxing and occasionally dangerous.

Q: *What are the keys to success to being a bartender?*

A: Don't abuse alcohol if you want to do this work successfully. I can't stress this enough. Another key to success is networking with other bartenders. You have to climb your own ladder of success in this industry. Many bartenders work at multiple places, and they can help get you in. Popular bars are more likely to hire a working bartender from another location if they are recommended by one of their employees. Many bartenders bounce from job to job until they find a bar that offers maximum return for their efforts.

You might want to consider attending a bartending or technical school or take a class or two on mixing drinks. A bartending certificate takes only a few months to obtain, and it's a good credential to have, particularly if you want to bartend at a high-end bar, hotel, or restaurant. Programs often include instruction on state and local laws and regulations, cocktail recipes, proper attire

▲ A course in bartending and mixology is a smart investment to landing that job.

and conduct, and stocking a bar. Some of these schools also help their graduates find jobs. In addition to attending school, if you want to work at a nightclub or trendy bar, you might want to take a one-day or online TIPs (training for intervention procedures) course, designed to show you how to prevent intoxication and manage intoxicated customers. As the number of liquor-related lawsuits continues to grow, bars and nightclubs are starting to require their bartenders to take a TIPs course.

Learn the Lingo

Here are a few words that bartenders throw around on the job:

- **Call drink** A drink in which the customer asks for a specific brand of alcohol by name; these are almost always more expensive than regular drinks.

- **Nightcap** A glass of wine or liquor ingested before bedtime.

- **Nip** A term of measurement used to describe a quarter of a bottle. In the old days, people were known to have "a nipper" of brandy or another liquor before bed.

- **On the rocks** An expression for serving a drink on ice cubes; contrasts with "neat," which calls for serving a liquor pure—with no water or ice.

- **Twist** A small piece of lemon or lime peel that is squeezed over a drink.

- **Proof** An American system for measuring alcohol content by volume. The proof of a liquor is always marked on the bottle and is twice the pure alcohol percentage of the distillation. For example, there is a particularly strong Bacardi line of rum called 151, which refers to the 151 proof of the liquor, or its containing more than 75 percent pure alcohol.

See what it's like to be a bartender.

Finding a Job

Thankfully, you don't need to be Tom Cruise in *Cocktail* to find work as a bartender. There is a preponderance of bartending jobs available in the United States. However, it's a popular profession, so jobs are often snatched up quickly. In order to snag one, you must be tenacious. Don't be afraid to walk into a bar or restaurant and hand the owner your résumé. It's important to remember that, since the job requires little or no training, how you appear in person is just as important as how you appear on paper. A sunny and difficult-to-rattle disposition goes a long way in bartending. If you are disinclined to drop into a restaurant or bar unannounced, you may find a bartending job by checking online or city bulletin boards and through word of mouth. Internet sites such as Craigslist.org and Monster.com are good resources. However, if you do decide to drop off your résumé, make sure you give it to the owner or bar manager instead of the current bartender, who might be reluctant to pass it along.

Tips for Success

- Talk 'em up. Although a friendly and winsome personality is technically not a job requirement, it certainly helps, particularly if you want to make good tips and develop a loyal clientele. Whenever you have some downtime, make an effort to chat with your customers at the bar and make sure that they are happy with their drinks.

- Know the law. Most important, be sure you know the state and local laws concerning the sale of alcoholic beverages. Serving liquor to a minor can result in the closing of a bar.

In some states you might also be responsible for the actions of an intoxicated customer who drinks on your premises.

Reality Check

Although there are a lot of fun aspects to bartending, the hours can be long and the work can be messy and physically tiring. Dealing with intoxicated patrons can be very challenging at times. Also, bartenders at some establishments are required to "upsell," meaning to push customers to buy additional drinks or appetizers. The selling aspect of this job is not for everyone.

LEARN MORE ONLINE

EXTREME BARTENDING
This is a fun and informative site that offers information on the latest mixing tricks and trends. It also provides valuable tips on how to find jobs in the field. http//:www.extreme bartending.com

AMERICAN HOTEL AND LODGING ASSOCIATION
This site has a great job search engine that's updated on a consistent basis and easy to use. http://www.ahla.com/index.asp

Related Jobs to Consider

Waiter/waitress or host/hostess. Like bartending, these jobs require you to work in similar environments and to be be fast, fastidious, and friendly. For a more complete description of what goes into waiting and hostessing, see Chapter 4.

Sommelier. After working as a bartender for a few years, some people become very passionate about wine. Sommeliers are wine experts who are hired by upscale restaurants to order wines and to help customers select wines that will complement their palates and their meals.

How to Move Up

• Create your own concoctions. Experimentation and innovation can go a long way in the bartending business, so don't be afraid to create and name your own drinks. Owners and managers are often impressed with **ingenuity**, and customers like to try a new house specialty drink.

- Take a class. If you decide you really enjoy bartending, get your bartending license and take at least one class in food service management and accounting. Alternatively, you might want to consider taking some culinary courses.

- Schmooze. The word may sound silly, but in the bartending business getting to know your customers may help you land a promotion or a better-paying job elsewhere, or connect you with an opportunity in some other area of your interests.

- Be a manager. Take on additional responsibilities for the restaurant or bar where you work, such as maintaining the staff schedule, and you are likely to be promoted to manager.

TEXT-DEPENDENT QUESTIONS

1. *What types of establishments do bartenders work in?*

2. *What personal qualities does a good bartender need and why?*

3. *How do you get trained in this field?*

4. *What is the "proof" system?*

RESEARCH PROJECTS

1. *The best way to find out if you'd like bartending as a career is to try it out. Although the drinking age is 21, in some states you can work as a bartender at age 18. If you're under 18, try finding work busing or waiting tables. You'll be able to find out if the restaurant environment is a good match for you. Also, some people transition from waiting to bartending positions.*

2. *Do some research on the various restaurants, bars, and hotels in your area, and decide what sort of an establishment you'd like to work in. Once you've found a few places that interest you, introduce yourself to the manager or owner.*

Floral Designer

Add color and happiness to others' lives. Design floral displays and bouquets. Design floral displays and bouquets.

WORDS TO UNDERSTAND

horticulture: the practice of garden cultivation and management.

persnickety: picky or hard to please.

wholesale: here, describes a company that sells goods to other companies, who then sell to customers.

Gertrude Stein once wrote, "A rose is a rose is a rose." Though this may be true for the average person, a florist knows there are more than 100 different wild rose species in the Northern Hemisphere alone. Florists are nature's salespeople. They cut live flowers and greenery and arrange them into beautiful displays. It's a wonderfully creative job that adds color and joy to people's lives. Nowadays, almost every major occasion in life calls for a flower display: weddings, funerals, promotions, prom nights, performances, Valentine's Day, and Christmas all involve flowers or greenery of some sort. According to analysts at Dun & Bradstreet, there are more than 13,000 independent florist shops in the United States. In addition, some florists work as part of larger businesses, such as supermarkets or **wholesale** distribution companies. There are about 55,000 floral designers, according to the U.S. Bureau of Labor Statistics.

◀ Working with an experienced floral designer is an excellent way to learn the trade.

▲ Local florists may get their tulips from a wholesale greenhouse such as this one.

Is This Job Right for You?

To find out if being a floral designer could be the right job for you, read each of the following questions and answer "Yes" or "No."

Yes	No		
Yes	No	1.	*Are you creative, and do you have an eye for color and composition?*
Yes	No	2.	*Are you patient and detail oriented?*
Yes	No	3.	*Are you passionate about flowers?*
Yes	No	4.	*Do you enjoy working with your hands?*
Yes	No	5.	*Would you enjoy learning about the qualities of hundreds of floral varieties?*
Yes	No	6.	*Are you comfortable working weekends and holidays?*
Yes	No	7.	*Do you work well under pressure?*
Yes	No	8.	*Are you friendly and personable?*
Yes	No	9.	*Can you work well both independently and with others?*
Yes	No	10.	*Can you interpret other's design needs and preferences?*

If you answered "Yes" to most or all of these questions, you may want to consider a career as a floral designer. To find out more about this job, read on.

What's the Work Like?

As a floral designer, you are required to be both an artist and a listener. When a customer walks in the store, a good florist will talk to the person to figure out how to convey just the right message with a floral arrangement. Once the right bouquet or display has been chosen, a florist must price the order and give the customer a time estimate. After this is accomplished, the florist can put together the arrangement. Florists may also receive written or online orders, which do not require customer contact. This is particularly common at large retail stores and Internet florists.

However, most florists today still work in small storefront shops with 10 or fewer employees.

> ## TALKING MONEY
>
> Floral designers earn a median annual income of about $25,850, according to 2016 data from the U.S. Bureau of Labor Statistics. However, those who manage their own stores often make substantially more.

Whether you're self-employed or working in a small florist shop, you will frequently work independently, so you should be a self-sufficient and disciplined worker. You will likely also handle large orders for weddings, caterers, or interior designers. These jobs often require florists to put in extra hours and to go onsite to arrange bouquets and floral displays. Seasoned florists are also asked to collaborate with interior designers on major design projects for hotels, restaurants, and private homes.

Who's Hiring?

- Small flower shops

- Florist chains

- Wholesalers

- Large grocery stores

- Online flower companies

Where Are the Jobs?

Although job environments in the floral industry vary, many florists still work in small, independently run shops with a strong repeat-client base. To supplement their store income, many florists also run gift shops or wedding consultation businesses.

If you aren't a self-employed florist or employed at an independent flower shop, you may work for a wholesale flower distribution company. Wholesale florists select different varieties of flowers and greenery and sell them to retail florists. This job requires an intimate knowledge of the industry, as well as a sharp eye.

In recent years, the Internet flower industry has also started to flourish, and as a result, a growing number of people are seeking employment in this area. As an Internet florist, your job is to create prearranged floral bouquets and displays. Although the job doesn't involve much creativity or collaboration, you won't have to deal with **persnickety** clients.

These days many people are picking up their flowers at large grocery chains. Florists also work designing and creating the arrangements at large distribution centers. However, these positions don't offer as many opportunities for self-expression.

A Typical Day

Here are the highlights of a typical day in a floral shop.

Brighten up the shop. Arrange a few fresh bouquets or topiaries for the storefront window. Once the shop is looking brighter, you'll want to prearrange a few fresh bouquets for customers who are in a hurry. The morning is also a good time to call distributors and schedule deliveries.

Dote on your customers. Chat with those who stop by the store to find out the reason they are shopping for flowers and what sort of flowers they appreciate. Once you know the occasion and the customer's likes and dislikes, you'll be able to arrange something unique and appropriate for them.

Clean up and close the store. After store hours, you'll need to close the register and sweep up any petals or leaves from the floor. Before leaving, it's always a good idea to see what deliveries are scheduled for the next day.

▲ As a florist with a storefront, you may have customers that stop in to shop. Ask lots of questions to see what arrangement would be right for the customer.

Start Preparing Now

- Pay attention in biology class! If you're no longer in school, take a botany or **horticulture** class. Most colleges offer horticulture courses, and some community centers have evening classes in botany or flower appreciation.

- Try finding part-time or volunteer work at a local florist. Even if you're just delivering flowers, you'll eventually learn the great arrangement for every occasion.

Training and How to Get It

On-the-job training is a good way to gain an understanding of the business. It's also the best way to develop your own style and figure out what particular type of floral design (funeral wreaths, topiaries, bouquets) suits you best. Floral design is one of the few design occupations that doesn't require a postsecondary education, so many florists are high school graduates who have a creative flair and an interest in the arts as well as nature.

However, those who do have formal training in floral design tend to have a leg up on the competition. If you're interested in opening your own store or becoming a floral designer, you might want to consider a floral school or a community college that awards certificates in floral design. These programs are usually inexpensive and can be completed in one year or less. Through them you'll learn the basics in floral design: the different species of flowers, their color and texture, cutting and taping techniques, and proper handling and care of flowers. Many programs will also teach you the elements of running your own floral business, from pricing to bookkeeping.

See what it's like to be a florist.

NOTES FROM THE FIELD

Floral arranger and store manager, Austin, Texas

Q: How did you get your job?

A: I had interviews with other floral shops, but ultimately I felt that the King Florist team would give me the opportunity to excel in the floral industry. When you're first starting out, it's important to interview with a lot of florists. Since most businesses are small, it's important to pick the work environment that suits you best. At King Florist, I started as a general staff member, and after two years of writing down orders and arranging flowers, I was promoted to shop manager.

Q: What do you like best about your job?

A: It's wonderful to be around flowers, and to use your creativity at the workplace every day. It's also nice to have a customer appreciate your work. People are often fascinated by the many ways in which we can present flowers, so I love seeing their reaction when they receive a bouquet that was created and designed just for them.

Q: What's the most challenging part of your job?

A: Dealing with new or demanding clients can sometimes be difficult. Also, when a potential client calls, you only have a few minutes to sell them on the fact that King Florist is a trusted name. Since flower shops are small and friendly, it's easy to forget that we are in the sales business. For some people, the selling part of the job can be difficult.

Q: What are the keys to success to being a florist?

A: Apart from strong customer service skills, the biggest key to success in this business is consistency and a distinguished style. If you consistently create floral designs that appeal to your clientele, and noticeably set you apart from the flower shop around the corner, you should be in business for a long time.

Learn the Lingo

Here are a few words that you're likely to hear on the job:

- **Oasis** Special foam used in flower arrangements. It retains water like a sponge and hydrates flowers for an extended period of time.

- **Topiary** Flowers or foliage trimmed into geometric shapes. The design often resembles miniature trees or animals.

- **Nosegays** Small, round bouquets that are composed of densely packed round flowers, greenery, and occasionally herbs. Nosegays are either wired or tied together.

Finding a Job

If you're interested in running your own floral business, start by going to your local flower district and have a look around. Once you feel familiar with the regional flowers and their pricing, consider buying several dozen different flowers, obtaining a wholesale license (license prices vary state by state but usually cost about $2 per day) and opening up a stand. If you don't have the clientele or the overhead to start your own store, this is the best way to make money and get to know your client base. If, on the other hand, you're interested in working on the corporate side of the industry, a number of online and wholesale flower companies now offer internships.

Tips for Success

- Since flowers are all about presentation, it's important to smile and present yourself in a pleasant way. A good florist knows the right flowers for the right occasion, and to pick the right bouquet or floral display, you need to be able to listen and interpret the needs of your client. After all, you wouldn't want to sell a Venus flytrap to a man who's about to propose.

- Learn about color—design books can be a good place to start. The color composition of a bouquet determines a lot of what it expresses.

Reality Check

Flowers may be pretty, but unfortunately, the same can't be said for the flower industry. Flower shops rely on word of mouth, and some clients take advantage of this fact. As a result, florists often have to go to great efforts to please and appease their clients.

▲ Creating a wedding bouquet is a high-visibility commission.

Related Jobs to Consider

Horticulture assistant. This occupation allows you to work with flora and fauna in nurseries or elsewhere. These workers usually have regular hours, but they are often laboring outdoors in hot weather for long periods of time.

Fashion designer. As with flower arranging, fashion design requires you to have a good eye for color and composition. However, fashion design is an extremely competitive area and typically requires more education.

How to Move Up

• Take a horticulture class at a local college or community center. At the very least, read books and watch videos on floral design and botany and start memorizing the many different species of flowers that are available through your wholesalers or locally.

- Learn all you can about the whole-sale flower distribution business. Even if you have no interest in working as a flower distributor, this is a great way to learn about the flower industry. Consider volunteering as an intern or taking a part-time job in this area to solidify your knowledge.

- Be quick to volunteer for additional responsibilities at your job. Come in during rush periods, be willing to fill in for others, and generally make yourself indispensable—especially with regard to management tasks.

- Take business courses at a local community college and learn all you can about running your own business or managing others.

LEARN MORE ONLINE

AMERICAN INSTITUTE OF FLORAL DESIGNERS (AIFD)

This is one of the best networking resources for florists. Their Web site tracks the latest floral trends and often features floral events, job opportunities, workshops, and symposia. http://www.aifd.org

FLOWERCHAT.COM

Flower Chat is a great site to visit if you are new to the industry and would like to speak with florists from around the country. It offers plenty of experts who are willing to field questions and help you get started. http://www.flowerchat.com

TEXT-DEPENDENT QUESTIONS

1. *What types of establishments hire florists?*

2. *How do you get trained in this field?*

3. *What is a topiary?*

4. *How can you move up in this field?*

▲ When you've landed your first job working for a florist, be sure to make yourself indispensable. Offer to work longer hours or make home deliveries.

RESEARCH PROJECTS

1. *Try out floral design for yourself. Borrow a few flower-arranging books from your local library or take a floral design class. Then buy an assortment of flowers and practice putting together handheld bouquets, corsages, or arrangements for containers. Once you've mastered the basics, you can move on to advanced concepts in floral design, such as horizontal, landscape, and waterfall style.*

2. *The ability to use color effectively is an essential part of every designer's job. Teach yourself about color theory by exploring sites like Color Matters (https://www.colormatters.com/) and Artyfactory (https://www.artyfactory.com/color_theory/color_theory.htm).*

Launderer or Dry Cleaner

Make clothes smell fresh and please customers. Expose yourself to fashion styles. Work in a social environment.

WORDS TO UNDERSTAND

couture: describes clothes that are made specifically to meet a particular client's requests.

solvent: a substance that can dissolve other substances.

telecommuting: using the Internet to work from home instead of in an office.

Being a dry cleaner is one of the most overlooked fashion-related careers. Though it may not be as glamorous as designing **couture** clothes, the work is steady, and there is a great demand for dry cleaners. People of almost every age and income use laundry and dry cleaning services, which is why such businesses can be found in virtually every American town and city. Moreover, there is more to dry cleaning than just removing stains and spots—a lot of hard work and responsibility goes into running a laundry and dry cleaning business.

As a dry cleaner, you are responsible for people's most cherished articles of clothing. You are also under a lot of deadlines. It is not uncommon for someone to come into the store with a tuxedo that needs to be cleaned by tomorrow or a tie that needs a stain removed for a dinner that evening.

◄ Keeping track of customers' clothing is job one for any dry cleaner. Tickets help but there needs to be a back-up system for customers who lose their tickets.

It's a demanding job, but there is a great amount of satisfaction involved. It's also relatively easy to start your own laundry and dry cleaning business. So if you're a careful worker who enjoys clothing and wants to run a small business, this may be the field for you.

Is This Job Right for You?

To find out if being a laundry or dry cleaning worker is a good fit for you, read each of the following statements and answer "Yes" or "No."

Yes	No	1. *Do you enjoy working with fabrics and cloth?*
Yes	No	2. *Are you good at budgeting your time?*
Yes	No	3. *Can you work weekends or evenings?*
Yes	No	4. *Are you capable of being on your feet all day?*
Yes	No	5. *Are you a strong, independent worker?*
Yes	No	6. *Are you free of allergies to chemicals or perfumes, or can you manage them?*
Yes	No	7. *Might you be interested in running a business?*
Yes	No	8. *Do you have an appreciation for fashion?*
Yes	No	9. *Are you a neat person who values cleanliness?*
Yes	No	10. *Are you friendly, and could you attract a loyal client base?*

If you answered "Yes" to most of the questions, you may be well suited to work as a dry cleaner. To find out more about this profession, read on.

What's the Work Like?

As a laundry or dry cleaning worker, your responsibility is to launder, clean, dye, and press an ongoing stream of articles—from clothing, linens, and bedding to curtains, drapes, and rugs. Though this may seem like a simple task, dry cleaning is actually a rather intricate process. One of the biggest myths about dry cleaning is that the process is entirely dry. Actually, dry cleaning uses a variety of different non-water-based **solvents** to remove stains and clean clothes. The solvent is placed inside a dry cleaning machine, which acts as both a washing machine and dryer.

As a dry cleaner, it is your job to monitor the machine and adjust the temperatures according to the color and fabric of the materials. It is also your job to ensure that a customer's item is not lost or misplaced. Like most jobs in human services, customer satisfaction is essential to the business. In addition to being fast and efficient, you must also be friendly and courteous. Whether it's an expensive designer garment or someone's favorite pair of blue jeans, clients trust their dry cleaner to remove spots, repair hems, and make sure those garments are looking their best. The personal component of the job is particularly important if you're the manager or owner of the business.

Laundry and dry cleaning stores are steady and reliable business enterprises, which is why many budding business owners open dry cleaning businesses. There is a strong entrepreneurial element in the laundry and dry cleaning industry. Not only can you open a store almost anywhere, as the owner you get to decide what services to offer. Offering additional services, such as tailoring, same-day home delivery, or environmentally "green" cleaning processes is a good way for owners to separate themselves from the competition.

▲ Pressing and folding clothing after it has been washed is a good starting job at a dry cleaning store.

Laundry and dry cleaning establishments usually have one manager and at least three employees. There is also an owner, but in many cases the owner and manager are one and the same. It's important to know that a lot of laundry and dry cleaning businesses are family run. This often close-knit family dynamic can create a warm and intimate work environment for some, but it can also make others feel like an outsider.

As for your clientele, it's usually very diverse. Though office workers tend to need shirts pressed and skirts cleaned on a more regular basis, almost everyone has a need for dry cleaning at some point. Thus, as a dry cleaner, you'll be able to meet and serve a diverse group of customers.

TALKING TRENDS

As long as people need to wear clean clothes, there will always be launderers and dry cleaners. However, there are some broad trends that are slowing the growth of jobs in the field. Workplace trends like **telecommuting** and the popularity of "business casual" dress have cut into the need for white-collar workers to constantly have clothes dry cleaned. Also, increasing numbers of fabrics are now washable at home, rather than requiring the services of a dry cleaner. As of 2016, there were over 180,000 laundry and dry-cleaning workers in the United States—a large number, but one that is not expected to increase dramatically. The next frontier in this field is likely to be "green" dry cleaning that reduces the number of dangerous chemicals involved.

Who's Hiring?

- A small business owner
- Hotels
- Nursing homes and hospitals
- Yourself

Where Are the Jobs?

One of the best parts about being in the laundry and dry cleaning business is that you can find work wherever you live. Laundry and dry cleaning establishments are found throughout the nation, so if you want to settle down in a small town, just find a business partner or gather up

NOTES FROM THE FIELD

Dry cleaning business manager, Bloomfield, New Jersey

Q: *How did you get your job?*

A: My parents owned a dry cleaning business, so it was a way for me to spend time with my parents. I would stop by and help out after school and on Saturdays. That's how it started. As I grew up, I just took over the business from my parents.

Q: *What do you like best about your job?*

A: Dry cleaners attract local business, so as a dry cleaner, you get to know your neighbors. You would be amazed at how much you learn about people and life just by speaking with customers and taking care of their clothes on a regular basis.

Q: *What's the most challenging part of your job?*

A: Trying to remove stains from customer's clothes—it is amazing what people get on their clothes. They also think that dry cleaners can remove every stain, but sometimes that's just not possible, particularly if you have a wine or ink stain on a white, absorbent fabric.

Q: *What are the keys to success to being a dry cleaner?*

A: The three main keys to success in this business are quality, maintenance, and customer service. High-quality dry cleaning makes clothes look and feel like you just bought them. Equipment maintenance is also essential. If one of your machines breaks down you cannot do any work until it's fixed. The final key to success is customer service. Without good customer service, you are bound to fail in this or any other business.

some money on your own. Or, if you crave the culture and entertainment that places like Los Angeles or New York have to offer, you can make a decent living running your own laundry and dry cleaning shop in a big city.

One thing to keep in mind is that laundry and dry cleaning establishments typically make most of their money during the evening and on weekends, so weekend and evening shifts are pretty standard. Some managers or owners rotate schedules so that employees do not continuously work nights or weekends, but this can cause sleep disorders or other aggravations.

A Typical Day

Ever wonder what a dry cleaner does with your clothes once you leave? As a dry cleaner, you'll spend a great deal of your day doing the following.

Tag and sort. You'll affix a small identification tag to the customer's clothing. The tag helps distinguish the clothes, and so it remains attached to the clothing during the entire dry-cleaning cycle.

Run the machines. You or a colleague will put the clothing into a machine to be cleaned with a powerful solvent. Most modern machines are a washer, extractor, and dryer all in one and can hold between 20 to 100 pounds of clothing or fabric.

Post-spot those stains! This process involves using a variety of equipment and chemicals to get particular stains out. Water-based stains such as tomato sauce are removed using steam

▲ After the clothing has been washed, and pressed, it is hung on a hanger and packaged in a plastic wrapping. It is then tagged and placed on a rotating belt organized by ticket number.

or wet-side chemicals. Other stains (grease or nail polish) are removed using solvents or dry-side chemicals.

Finish up. To get a garment or item is ready for the customer, you either press, fold, and package, or oversee this process.

Start Preparing Now

- Take chemistry classes to familiarize yourself with the properties of the chemicals used in the dry cleaning process.

- Look for part-time or week-end work at a local laundry or dry cleaning establishment. Even if you're just pressing shirts or sweeping up lint, you'll get a good sense of how the business works.

Watch the dry cleaning process as it happens.

Training and How to Get It

On-the-job training is the best way to break into this business. Although employers prefer applicants to have previous work experience, laundry and dry cleaning managers routinely hire inexperienced workers. Often an owner or manager will have you shadow another employee for a week, so you can learn the basic procedures. After that, you're on your own. College degrees, business management experience, or dry-cleaning training certificates will definitely set you apart from the competition, but a high school diploma is all that's really needed in order to work at a dry cleaning establishment.

Though most states require dry cleaning businesses to be certified, employees typically do not need any form of certification. There are, however, week- or month-long courses that teach the basic principles of the dry cleaning process, stain removal, and finishing procedures on pants, coats, and skirts. These courses also cover some business basics, such as assembly and invoicing as well as regulations and care labeling.

If you're planning on opening a laundry or dry cleaning shop someday, it's a good idea to take courses in both business and fabric maintenance. Dry cleaning also deals with hazardous chemicals, which can pollute the environment if employees are not careful. In an effort to keep our air clean, a lot of states have now imposed environmental training regulations. These courses will give you a brief history of dry cleaning solvents, and teach you how to prevent toxic leaks and environmental damage through recordkeeping and rigorous maintenance checks. Regardless of whether your state requires you to take environmental courses, it is essential that you study up on the hazardous effects of perchloroethylene (perc) and the other solvents used during the cleaning process.

Learn the Lingo

Here are a few words you're likely to hear as a laundry or dry cleaning worker:

- **Perchloroethylene (perc)** This solvent is the standard for cleaning performance. It's a very aggressive cleaner that can cause color loss if it is not used properly and at the right temperature.

- **Pretreatment** This is a technique in which a cleaner uses chemicals to remove or minimize a stain before the dry cleaning process.

- **The basket** Also known as the washing/extracting chamber, the basket is the core of the dry cleaning machine. It consists of a shell, which holds the solvent, and a rotating drum, which can hold between 20 to 100 pounds of garments.

- **Filter cake (aka muck)** This accumulates on the surface of the lint filter. The muck must be removed once per day, and then filtered to recover any solvent trapped in the muck.

Finding a Job

To find a job in the laundry or dry cleaning business, call or stop by businesses for whom you think you'd like to work. Remember, there are dry cleaning businesses in almost every town, so you'll probably have at least several options. Be sure to research all the stores in your surrounding area. Remember that dry cleaners prefer efficient, friendly, and presentable people, so press your shirt before going into an interview, and be sure to greet everyone with a smile. Most facilities will offer training, so you needn't worry about your experience level. Dry cleaning stores have a consistent turnover rate, so if you can't find a job at your favorite dry cleaner, check back every few weeks or months. Another point to keep in mind is that dry cleaners are often busier on weekends and during the holiday season, so asking for part-time work during these times is an option.

Tips for Success

- Look professional. People launder and dry clean their clothes because they want to look clean and presentable; so as the dry cleaner, it is important for you to look polished and presentable too.

- Don't cut corners. Equally important is the quality of your services, which depends largely on the degree to which you control the dry cleaning machine's filter, solvent condition, and moisture. Therefore it is important to pay careful attention to the machines and perform maintenance work on them when necessary.

Reality Check

Laundry and dry cleaning establishments are often hot and noisy, so if you are looking for a quiet work environment, this may not be the job for you. In addition, injuries are not uncommon because some of the solvents used are flammable and the machines operate at high speeds.

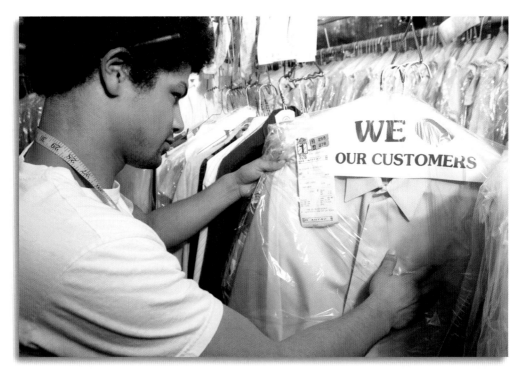

▲ Although employers prefer applicants to have previous work experience, laundry and dry cleaning managers routinely hire workers with no experience.

Related Jobs to Consider

Cobbler. Cobblers repair shoes and work in the same sorts of small storefronts as favored by dry cleaners. The customer contact may be less regular because shoes stay fixed longer than clothes stay clean, but many find this old-world craft a very fulfilling occupation.

Upholsterer. Upholsterers work closely with customers in repairing furniture and making it from scratch. They work a lot with their hands, and have to be competent with numbers as there are many separate pieces that must come together to form a whole.

LEARN MORE ONLINE

DRYCLEANING & LAUNDRY INSTITUTE
This Web site offers vital and up-to-date information about the garment-cleaning industry. For institute members, there are forums, contact lists, online seminars, and invitations to conferences. http://www.dlionline.org/

NATIONAL CLEANERS ASSOCIATION (NCA)
This is a great trade organization that services garment-cleaning businesses both large and small. Headquartered in New York City, the NCA offers scholarships and can put you in touch with industry experts. Check your state association's site as well. http://www.nca-i.com

GREENEARTH CLEANING
This site offers information on environmentally cleaner, perc-free dry cleaning processes, as well as other information, and its "green" dry cleaners by city and state. http://www.greenearthcleaning.com

How to Move Up

- One of the best ways to establish yourself is to take part in community activities. You'd be amazed at how much business you can drum up just by being an active member of the community. If you own your own business, your profits can be increased substantially by adding new services, such as boxing and storing, home delivery, alteration services, and coin machine laundering.

- Once you know the business, another option is to open several dry cleaning outlets with a central locale for the dry cleaning processes.

TEXT-DEPENDENT QUESTIONS

1. *What are some of the tasks that dry cleaners perform?*

2. *What is a typical day like?*

3. *How many people currently work in laundry and dry-cleaning jobs?*

4. *What are some related jobs you might consider?*

RESEARCH PROJECTS

1. *Each laundry and dry-cleaning establishment is slightly different. Research some of the specialized services, such as bridal-gown cleaning, corporate dry cleaning, and "green" processes, and decide which ones interest you most.*

2. *Find out more about "green" dry cleaning by checking out pages on Green America (https://www.greenamerica.org/green-living/green-dry-cleaning) and The Spruce (https://www.thespruce.com/what-is-green-dry-cleaning-2145936). You might also search online for "green dry cleaning in my area"; if you can, visit the establishments and talk to them about how and why they are switching to more "green" processes.*

Baseball Umpire

Watch the games up close. Be in the middle of the action. Make the calls that count.

WORDS TO UNDERSTAND

clinic: here, a short course on a specific subject.

isolating: describes a situation that causes a person to be (or simply feel) separated from others.

regimen: a regular program, such as an exercise regimen.

Behind every great baseball player, there's always an umpire. Truly. Umpires stand behind the bases, and although they might not hit the winning run, they're always the ones to call it. The fate and integrity of every baseball game rests on the umpire's shoulders, which is why some of the more notable "umps" have been inducted into the Baseball Hall of Fame. Success at this level requires good judgment, thick skin, and a love of the game.

At times, being an umpire can be a thankless job, but if you can look beyond the boos and the occasional peanut throw, there's nothing quite like seeing a home run from behind home plate. It's a demanding job, both mentally and physically, but if you enjoy sports and like to call all the shots, you could be one of the lucky few who do it for a living.

◀ The integrity of every baseball game rests on the umpire's shoulders, which is why some of the more notable "umps" have been inducted into the Baseball Hall of Fame.

Is This Job Right for You?

To find out if being a professional umpire is the right job for you, read each of the following questions and answer "Yes" or "No."

Yes	*No*	**1.**	*Are you a serious baseball fan?*
Yes	*No*	**2.**	*Did you grow up playing or watching sports?*
Yes	*No*	**3.**	*Are you highly exact and detail oriented?*
Yes	*No*	**4.**	*Can you handle stressful situations?*
Yes	*No*	**5.**	*Do you like making judgment calls?*
Yes	*No*	**6.**	*Would your friends call you extremely fair minded and morally sound?*
Yes	*No*	**7.**	*Do you have 20/20 vision with or without corrective lenses?*
Yes	*No*	**8.**	*Do you have good communication skills?*
Yes	*No*	**9.**	*Are you a team player?*
Yes	*No*	**10.**	*Would you like to travel for work?*

If you answered "Yes" to most of the questions, you may have what it takes to be an umpire. To find out more about this profession, read on.

What's the Work Like?

We all know that umpires call all the shots, but we often forget just how much pressure and responsibility come with that. Every foul, run, hit, or strike that is made this year will be called by one of the major league's 68 umpires, and unlike referees in American football, the umpire's judgment call is final. The job carries a lot of responsibility, and with it a lot of temptation, which is why umpires must be levelheaded.

As a professional umpire, your primary job is to encourage sportsmanship and to promote fair and safe play. Though this may seem like simply a matter of strong morals and a positive attitude, in fact it takes a tremendous level of skill and experience to be

TALKING MONEY

According to 2016 data from the U.S. Bureau of Labor Statistics, the median annual earnings for umpires and other sports officials is $25,660. However, salaries for umpires in Major League Baseball start at about $120,000 and can go as high as $350,000. Be aware, however, that jobs in the Major League are very hard to get.

able to call a play. First you need to know how to position yourself according to the play. You should know approximately where a ball is going to land before the hitter even connects with the ball.

The home plate umpire is generally said to have the hardest job, which is the reason he or she is given the title umpire-in-chief. It's not uncommon for the plate ump to make

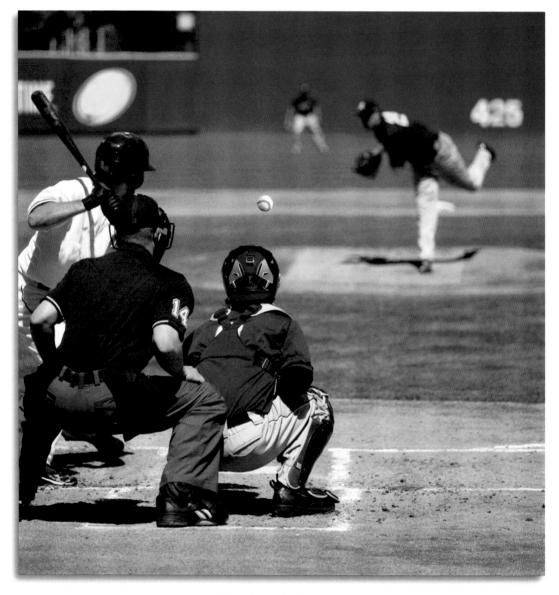

▲ An umpire's office is home plate.

over 300 calls in one night—and to be able to do that with accuracy, you need to have a lot of experience and training. Most umpires come into the majors after having worked for 8 to 12 years in the minor leagues.

Like athletes and coaches, umpires chose this profession because they have a love for the game. However, a thorough knowledge of the rule book is what matters most on the field. You may think you know baseball, but there are countless rules that even avid sports fans might

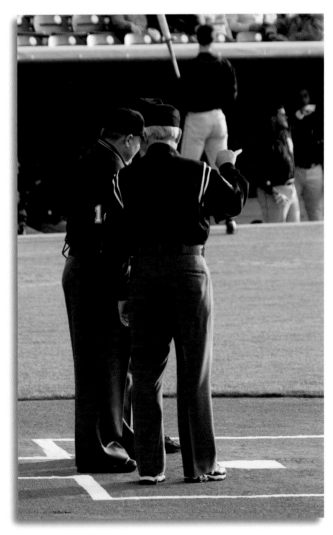

▲ There is a very low turnover rate for umpires in the major leagues, so everyone really gets a chance to know each other.

not be aware of. Take this scenario: There's a player on first who's running on a pitch. The catcher throws the ball to second, but mid-throw his elbow hits the umpire's mask. The ball sails into centerfield, and the runner starts heading for third, but just as he reaches the base the centerfielder tags him.

While most would say that the runner is out, according to the Major League Baseball rule book, he gets to return to first because only a catcher's throw can retire a runner. Umpires must be able to make a technical call like this within seconds of the play. It's a job that requires a surprising amount of brainpower.

In addition to the mental workout, umpires also need to be in good physical shape. Depending on where an umpire is positioned, he or she is either squatting to call a pitch, ducking to miss a fly ball, or hustling to see a play. With all this action, it's important to stay in shape, particularly now that the leagues require umpires to pass an annual physical that includes a stress treadmill test and a squat test, as well an eye and orthopedic examination and a concussion baseline test.

One element of the umpire's life that most people associate with the players is the element of camaraderie. Few people realize that umpires have their own sense of team spirit. Umpires in both the minors and the majors work in crews. During away games, these crews often travel and eat together.

There is a very low turnover rate for umpires in the major leagues, so everyone really gets a chance to know each other. By contrast, there are more umpires in the minor leagues and the turnover rate is much higher, so it can be harder to create meaningful bonds. There's also a lot of competition in the minors as every umpire is vying for the same spot in the majors, but if you're good at what you do, you'll rise in the ranks with other talented umpires and make friends along the way.

Umpires stick together in part because they share a passion for the game but also because being an umpire can sometimes be **isolating** and exhausting. In addition to all the traveling, umpires often have to contend with disgruntled fans, players, and coaches. Sports games have the ability to bring out some pretty heated emotions in even the most passive people. During intense

TALKING TRENDS

Umpires and referees held around 21,000 jobs in 2016. Many professional umpires make good money working for colleges and universities. In addition, there are thousands of umpires who work part time.

games or when two rival teams are playing, coaches and players have been known to verbally and even physically abuse umpires just because they didn't agree with a call.

Who's Hiring?

- Little League teams

- College and high school teams

- Minor League Baseball

- Major League Baseball

Where Are the Jobs?

An umpire's office is home plate. Schools and Little Leagues, Major and Minor League Baseball all have need of umpires. Whether the backstop is in a community park or Yankee Stadium, the umpire will have traveled to get there, even if from just across town. Usually the umpire will change into game gear in a locker room at the stadium. When the competition ends, the umpire hits the showers and heads for a meal and some downtime (just like a player, an umpire needs a healthful **regimen** to stay fresh for the season). Although the work takes place outside, it is usually under conditions that are comfortable for a person in a short-sleeved shirt or a light sweater. Sunblock, though, should find a place in the umpire's toiletries bag, given all the time spent working in exposed areas and traveling. In the off-season, an umpire may pursue professional development through a program that would typically be offered at an educational campus. Most would also have to spend a little office time to track invoices and cultivate future work.

A Typical Day

Here are the highlights of a typical day as a major league umpire.

Prepare with ritual. You're playing Arizona, and it's an away game. Like athletes, umpires keep a very strict schedule and are often prone to superstitions. You arrive at the stadium at your usual time—exactly two hours before game time—and after sharing a laugh with the crew and putting on your lucky pair of socks, everyone goes over the assignments.

Work the plate. You're the home-plate umpire, so even before the anthem, your head is in the game. Everything is running smoothly and you're making quick and decisive calls, but at the bottom of the eighth inning things get ugly. Arizona is behind by one, and you call a controversial strike that results in the end of the inning. The Arizona manager goes ballistic and throws a bucket of water in your direction. Following a consultation between the umpires, the manager is ejected from the game.

Wrap up post-game. After squatting behind the plate for 285 pitches, your team wins. Before returning to the umpire locker room to review the game, you should report the

▲ An umpire ejects a player from the game after the player gets rowdy due to a controversial call.

NOTES FROM THE FIELD

*Former Major League Baseball umpire (28 years)
and umpiring school owner,* Kissimmee, Florida

Q: *How did you get started?*

A: Like most umpires, I started as a player when I was 14 years old. My league at the time hosted a tournament of out-of-town teams, and they needed umpires. Since I was a catcher, the league's umpire-in-chief thought I would make a good plate umpire. My first day, I worked five games, and I enjoyed the experience so much that soon after I began umpiring on the days that I wasn't playing. Before long I was enjoying the umpiring more than the playing. I paid my way through college umpiring youth leagues, high school, and college ball. Upon graduation, I decided to give professional umpiring a try, so I went to umpire school and graduated at the top of my class. From there, I went on to enjoy a 32-year career in professional baseball, 28 in the major leagues.

Q: *What do you like best about your job?*

A: The spontaneity. When you walk onto the field for a game, you have no idea what's in store. I have worked the longest game in major league history (8 hours and 7 minutes), and I have worked no-hitters. I once worked three years without having to eject a player, and then I've had to eject five in one game. Tough situations and rough weather conditions also keep the job interesting. I've worked April games in the snow, and I've worked games in 125-degree weather. There is no script in baseball. Every game is a new and different melodrama.

Q: *What's the most challenging part of your job?*

A: The most challenging part of the job is staying motivated during the lulls and slow spots of a baseball game. If you do not talk to yourself and stay prepared, you are likely to make a mistake. Also, for professional umpires, being on the road a lot can make it difficult to concentrate.

Q: *What are the keys to success to being an umpire?*

A: **The first key is understanding your responsibilities. Knowing your specific duties and how they are divided among you and your crew is paramount. The second key is recognizing play possibilities. Once the ball is pitched, a multitude of things can happen. Reacting to the appropriate cues will enable you to acquire the proper position and make the correct call. Lastly, success is developing the proper mindset. Though you may not have a multimillion-dollar contract like some of the players, you should be just as proud of what you do. Without umpires there could be no game.**

ejection to the league president, who is in charge of doling out penalties. If your back or knees hurt from squatting, you opt for a treatment from one of the sports physicians. Otherwise, you shower in the locker room and head back to the hotel to rest before getting up and doing it all over again.

Start Preparing Now

- Study the umpire rule book, work out regularly, and watch as many games as possible.

- Get in touch with a minor or major league umpire in your area, so you can gain personal insight into what an umpire's life is like. Volunteer with the umps if you can.

- Contact a little league association, and volunteer to be an umpire for a local league.

Training and How to Get It

To break into the clubby world of professional umpires it takes a lot of hard work, discipline, and training. Academically speaking, a high school diploma is all that's required of you, but if you want to work in the majors, you must attend a training school accredited by the Professional Baseball Umpire Corp. (PBUC). The Jim Evans Academy in Kissimmee, Florida, and the Harry Wendelstedt School in Ormond Beach, Florida, are the gold standards in the industry. Both offer a highly competitive, five-week training course during baseball's off-season.

During training, you'll learn everything from hand signaling to the philosophy of umpiring. In addition to classroom work, there is a heavy physical component to most training programs. You'll receive instruction on the two-person umpiring system, and be asked to perform intense two-person drills. You'll also do a lot of plate work in the batting cage, but the most challenging aspect is the simulation of real games, also known as trial by fire. During these sessions student umpires face unusual situations, where they are forced to make calls and defend them against complaints from instructors pretending to be coaches, managers, and players. This method of instruction is meant to steel the nerves and strengthen the student's resolve. It's an important component of the training because managers keep track of the umpires, and when they see a new ump on the field, they often test their limits.

Other training includes angle-and-distance drills and pitch-calling drills, in which mirrors, measuring sticks, and video cameras are often employed for accuracy.

Finally, let's not forget your own physical training. While the athletes may be the ones sprinting for the ball or rounding the bases, the umpire is never too far behind. In order to have success on the field, you need to work out daily and live a healthy lifestyle.

Learn the Lingo

Here are some words that you're likely to hear as a professional umpire:

- **Adjudged** This is the official word for an umpire's decision.

- **Blues** Referees are sometimes referred to as blues because their uniforms are often blue in color.

- **Dead ball** This is a ball that is out of play because of a legally created temporary suspension of play.

- **Overslide** When an offensive player slides to a base with such momentum that he loses contact with the base.

Finding a Job

Although competition is stiff in the umpiring field, there are plenty of part-time jobs available for beginners looking to gain experience— though typically for very little or no pay. If you're still in high school, the Little Leagues are a great place to volunteer. And if you contact your regional Little League headquarters and sign up for a two- or four-day umpire **clinic**, you'll

▲ If you think the major leagues may be too much for you, or if you want to get some practice in, being an umpire for the Little Leagues may be the perfect job for you!

be on the field in no time. For high school athletics, you'll need to register with a state agency and pass an exam on the rules of the game before you can start umpiring. Contact the National Federation of State High School Associations (NFHS, http://www.nfhs.org) for information on openings in your area.

Once you've gained enough experience in the field, you can start thinking about college umpiring. This can be a competitive environment, but unlike the little leagues or high school athletics, you are paid a decent salary. College umpires must be certified by an official training school and be evaluated during a probationary period. If you do well at the college level, you will be admitted into the minors, where both the talent and the pay are greater.

The minor leagues are divided into four levels: rookie, short-season, long-season and advanced "A." Depending on your competency, you will start in the rookie or short-season league, and rise through the ranks until you make it to the majors. Although there are a lot of people vying for a small number of positions, professional umpires have a very high retention rate, so if you work hard and make it into the professional leagues, you're set for life.

Tips for Success

- Calling all the shots doesn't make you a hot shot. As an umpire, you have a surprising amount of authority and power on the field, which is the reason it's important to keep your ego in check. The best umpires are humble, accurate, and unbiased.

See what it's like to be an umpire.

- Always keep your eye on the ball while it's in play. It is more important to know just where a fly ball fell, or a thrown ball finished up, than whether a runner missed a base.

Reality Check

Nowadays, with the advent of technologies like instant replay and slow-motion cameras, an umpire's accuracy rate needs to be near perfect. In order to make it to the big leagues, almost all of your calls must be on the money.

Related Jobs to Consider

Coach. This is a sports job that requires you to be a confident decision maker. However, unlike umpires, coaches devise strategies instead of making calls. They also form intense bonds with the players on their team, and often have rivalries with other coaches in their league.

Fitness instructor. With this profession, there is an emphasis on being physically fit and active, and as with umpiring, the job requires a lot of energy, enthusiasm, and leadership skills.

How to Move Up

- Unlike minor league ballplayers, who are often recruited by the majors after only two seasons, umpires typically work in the minors for seven to ten years before they can be considered for the majors. To move up, you've got to be physically fit, work well with others, and have a high accuracy rate. Punctuality and appearance are also taken very seriously in this profession. In umpire school, being early, rather than on time, is stressed, and everyone receives instruction on how to clean a uniform. One umpire named Bill McGowan was inducted into the Baseball Hall of Fame for having gone 16 years without missing one inning. McGowan umpired 2,541 consecutive games; if you can do even half as many, you're guaranteed to move up in the ranks.

LEARN MORE ONLINE

MAJOR LEAGUE UMPIRES

This site provides you with a bevy of insider information on the umpire lifestyle. It includes blogs, statistics, and news updates on umpires. It also gives you tips on how to become an umpire. http://www.majorleagueumpires.com/

JIM EVANS ACADEMY OF PROFESSIONAL TRAINING

Jim Evans is one of the two accredited umpire training schools that you'll need to attend if you plan on becoming a professional umpire. The site explains their program philosophy and guides you through the application process. http://www.umpireacademy.com

MINOR LEAGUE BASEBALL

This site offers great information on umpiring in the major and minor leagues. It also has a lot of information on the PBUC. http://www.milb.com/index.jsp

TEXT-DEPENDENT QUESTIONS

1. *How many umpires are there in Major League Baseball?*

2. *What are some other places umpires work, beyond the major league?*

3. *What are some related jobs you might consider?*

RESEARCH PROJECTS

1. • *When watching games, try to think like an umpire. Just as good players rely on videos to study opposing pitchers and hitters, the best umpires frequently review game calls. The more you know about the game, the better your chances are of succeeding, so hit the rule books and study every game.*

2. • *Calling a game in the Major Leagues is the ultimate dream of most umpires, but it's not an easy road to get there. You can read more about what it's like by checking out memoirs such as* They Called Me God *by Doug Harvey,* Planet of the Umps *by Ken Kaiser, and* Called Out But Safe *by Al Clark.*

▲ Home plate umpire is considered the hardest job, which is why he or she is given the title umpire-in-chief.

INDEX

PHOTO CREDITS